THE DEFENCE OF WESTERN EUROPE

Also edited by John C. Garnett
THEORIES OF PEACE AND SECURITY

THE DEFENCE OF
WESTERN EUROPE

*Papers Presented at the National Defence College,
Latimer, in September, 1972*

Edited by
John C. Garnett

Macmillan

First published 1974 by
THE MACMILLAN PRESS LTD
London and Basingstoke
Associated companies in New York
Dublin Melbourne Johannesburg and Madras

SBN 333 15068 6

Printed in Great Britain by
WESTERN PRINTING SERVICES LTD
Bristol

Contents

The views expressed in these papers are those of the authors. They do not necessarily reflect the opinions or policies of the Ministry of Defence or of any other department or agency of the British Government.

Foreword

by Major-General T. D. H. McMeekin, C.B., O.B.E.,
Commandant, National Defence College

The National Defence College first opened its doors to students in September 1971, its task being to train mid-career officers of the armed forces, and equivalent civil servants, for more senior posts in the direction of United Kingdom defence by giving them a firmly based understanding of the environment, problems and techniques of defence business. This was, and is, a considerable challenge to all concerned. Whatever success may so far have been achieved has certainly owed much to the many friends of the College, both Service and civilian, who helped us by coming to Latimer either to lecture to our students, to join in discussions with them, or just to see what we were doing and to advise us and to wish us well. We owe them all a great deal and are very conscious of our debt.

Indeed, they were principally in mind when we first considered the possibility of holding a Residential Seminar at the National Defence College shortly after the first course had ended. The subject we chose – Western European Defence – had of course been central to much of our work and study here at Latimer and will remain so for as far ahead as we can see.

It was also clearly one in which there was much more to be said than the course itself had allowed; and which, in the circumstances of the moment, seemed likely to be of dynamic interest to a number of those concerned in defence study and defence business generally whom we had it in mind to invite.

We hoped that many of our friends would welcome this opportunity to meet each other to discuss these problems together and, if this was the case, Latimer might provide a convenient and useful place in which to do so. Secondly, it seemed to me that if others – each with some special knowledge or experience of the study it concerned – were prepared to meet here in discussion, we, on the staff of the N.D.C., would certainly benefit and might learn much to pass on to those attending courses here in the future.

Preliminary inquiries led us to believe that a short Residential Session on these lines would be welcome and in due course it was clear that a number of distinguished contributors were prepared to read papers to it. At that point we began to think of a wider audience and the idea of this small book was first mooted.

I should like at this point to say a special word about the American contribution. Professor Wayne Wilcox very kindly gave us a paper on the United States commitment to Europe which, at the last moment, he was unfortunately prevented from presenting himself. We were thus the more fortunate that Professor Paul Seabury, who happened to be in London, was both able and willing to step in at short notice and present this paper to the Seminar. We are very grateful to him. We were also very glad to welcome to the National Defence College Professor Lewis Halle of the Graduate Institute of International Studies, Geneva, who made a most stimulating contribution to our discussions. He had been at one time himself a member of the staff of the United States National War College, and we were delighted to find him prepared to encourage a United Kingdom college with similar aims.

Our thanks are also due to Professor Laurence Martin, the Academic Consultant to this College, who was unfortunately unable – because of prior commitments in the United States – to join the Seminar itself, but who has kindly allowed us to include in this book the paper which he would have delivered if he had been able to be with us. I feel that it makes a particularly valuable contribution to the book, and those who were present at the Seminar will, I think, regret that we did not have the opportunity to discuss it on that occasion.

I hope therefore that these papers will be of interest and value to a wider audience and that, through the medium of this book, the work of the National Defence College itself may perhaps become better known. Indeed, it is at least part of our aim that this College should be able to play a useful, responsible and recognised part in the study of defence topics in the United Kingdom. To this end we hope that further opportunities may occur in the future – perhaps along the same lines – to promote contact and discussion between those inside and outside the government service, from the academic world and from industry, on topics of mutual interest in the defence field.

In conclusion I should like to thank all our guests and in particular all those who contributed papers. Finally, as Commandant I should like to record my thanks to those on the staff of the College whose hard work contributed to what was, I believe, generally considered to be an enjoyable and useful Seminar.

T. D. H. McMEEKIN

1
The Nixon Doctrine and Europe

LAURENCE MARTIN[*]

For all who are not thoroughgoing revisionists towards the history of the Cold War, European security has rested for the past quarter century on the American guarantee. This guarantee was issued between 1947 and 1949 as the Truman Doctrine evolved into the North Atlantic Treaty, the first alliance contracted by the United States since its creation in 1789. The guarantee was not, as is commonly assumed, an essentially nuclear one, for it antedated the full dawn of the nuclear age, preceding as it did the invention of the thermonuclear weapon and the emergence of nuclear 'plenty'. Rather, this guarantee constituted a promise that anyone who attacked the democracies of Western Europe would find himself at war with the United States, and the embodiment of the guarantee in a treaty was an attempt to provide a deterrent certainty of this consequence that had been wholly lacking at the outset of the two previous world wars.

But if this guarantee was not originally nuclear, the evolution of nuclear weapons and the failure of the West to provide a conventional balance to the Red Army quickly gave the American–European military relationship a primarily nuclear cast. One result was to change the balance between the European–American contributions to the common defence. The nuclear element, chiefly provided by the United States, became the essence of the alliance's defensive potential. The conventional element, to which European contributions were originally intended to be predominant, became mere auxiliaries to the basic deterrent posture. Troop levels ceased to be measured against a concrete and definable

[*] Professor of War Studies, King's College, University of London.

standard – the enemy order of battle – and were determined instead by the currency of various theoretical purposes: the 'tripwire', the 'hostage', the 'pause' and the 'flexible response'. Perhaps even more significantly, the evolution of intercontinental strategic weapons put the two super-powers in a position where each could threaten and hope to deter the other directly, without the use of West European real estate. Europe thus ceased to be a physical bulwark of American security and became instead the biggest domino in the world: a counter in a complex and debatable set of determinants of the super-power balance but no longer an integral part of American last-ditch defence.

While the underlying basis of the American–European relationship has thus been gradually evolving over a long period, the transformation has not been clear-cut or complete and still less have the logical consequences been generally perceived or accepted. In the past three or four years, however, new elements have entered the process and prompted a new round in the constant process of revaluation. In particular there have been important changes in the Soviet–American relationship that conditions the whole Atlantic partnership and in the basic American perception of what security requires.

One of the chief sources of this reappraisal has been the phenomenon usually referred to as nuclear parity. The term is perhaps not the most felicitous, for it is not so much a particular quantitative balance that underlines the change in American strategic perspectives as the rather belated recognition of mutual vulnerability between the super-powers. Such a mutual vulnerability appears to have been the ultimate purpose behind Robert McNamara's policies as Secretary of Defence, but the emergence of improved and promising technologies for ballistic missile defence, multiple warheads and improved missile accuracy reopened the prospect that such mutual vulnerability and consequent deterrence might be attainable only by a costly and dynamic arms race. It is in an effort to avoid this expense that the super-powers have entered the SALT negotiations and concluded the initial strategic arms limitation agreement. While this achievement has done something to delimit the terms of competition and may, but by no means certainly will, curb expenditure on strategic arms, it also constitutes a formal recognition that mutual vulnerability is indeed all that the super-powers can achieve vis-à-vis each other. This recognition has profound implications for American alliance policy, although the full logical conclusions may not be translated into practical diplomatic consequences. In particular, the American threat to resort to strategic nuclear weapons, if need be, in defence of the allies of the United States looks increasingly threadbare.

No Gaullist-like alarm has spread through the alliance, because the present permissive atmosphere of détente makes most politicians and almost all taxpayers disbelieve that a serious challenge to security will in fact arise. To those few who bother to analyse the situation it seems very probable that even the remote possibility that the United States would honour its obligations to the point of strategic nuclear action is a more than sufficient deterrent to Soviet aggression at a time when Soviet motive and inclination to run risks seem small. Nevertheless, if most Europeans tend to discount the implications of the Soviet–American strategic deadlock for American alliance policy, there are signs that President Nixon does not. This is clearly one of the difficulties he had in mind when, defining the purpose of American nuclear strategy as 'the maintenance of forces adequate to prevent us and our allies from being coerced', he went on to warn that 'I must not be – and my successors must not be limited to the indiscriminate mass destruction of enemy civilians as the sole response to challenges'. As it has developed so far, SALT pushes the United States precisely towards such a position.

Parallel to the recognition of the strategic deadlock has come the process of American disillusionment with foreign policy, and with the role of military force, engendered by the Vietnam war. Whether or not American diplomacy can snatch some political success, the war has certainly not done much to enhance the American public's regard for the military establishment or to reinforce their enthusiasm for military solutions to national problems. As is so often the case, military failure has been mitigated by rethinking the conception of foreign policy that once justified the war. Thus there has been an eager tendency to question whether any substantial American interests are at stake in Asia, and this questioning has spilt over a little on to the evaluation of American commitments in Europe. At the same time there has been an equal tendency towards scepticism as to whether any real threat is posed to American interests by the one-time villains of the piece, China, the Soviet Union and 'international Communism', and towards the conclusion that even if those powers pursue purposes inimical to the United States, the evidence is that they will enjoy as little success in trying to make firm imperial extensions of influence as the United States has done.

The desire to downgrade the necessity for American military intervention overseas has been reinforced, of course, not merely by the desire to bring home the troops on humane grounds, but also to reduce military expenditure so as to release more of the disposable Federal budget for domestic concerns. The budgetary benefits to be secured from merely running down the Vietnam war have, however, been largely absorbed and henceforth cuts can be made only in the so-called baseline force levels of pre-Vietnamese military effort.

Thus the pressures on resources, disillusionment with the war and the reconsideration of national interests have all combined to bring about the desire for a lower profile and a lower level of overseas effort encapsulated in the Nixon Doctrine. In both its origins and its implications the Nixon Doctrine is primarily concerned with Asia. Europe has a favoured position. Whereas the Asians are told that American military intervention is likely to come only if extreme threats arise and that the normal vicissitudes of subversion and limited war will have to be dealt with by indigenous governments, albeit with some American material aid and perhaps occasional offshore military support, Europe has been assured that American force levels will be maintained unless some agreed and balanced reductions can be negotiated with the Soviet Union. Moreover, while in one respect the rather self-conscious *Realpolitik* of the Nixon–Kissinger combination implies a downgrading of Europe by its emphasis on a pentagonal multi-polar world in which Europe, Russia, China and Japan would be so many pieces on the diplomatic board, at other times the theme of a special relationship between the two Atlantic partners still makes an appearance in American exhortations. The generation of post-war American statesmen who were instinctive Atlanticists has largely passed from power, but fortunately for Europe one of their number still inhabits the White House and has taken himself a latter-day disciple.

Nevertheless, Europe is in no position to bask in American favour. Quite apart from the fact that any peculiarly European bias in President Nixon's outlook is clearly a wasting asset, the Nixon Administration's own principles are ambiguous. In American strategy the catchword is 'sufficiency'. This is an ambiguous phrase well worthy of an administration that has bemused its audience by a flood of delphic policy documents. Sufficiency can imply a limitation of military effort to those who deplore previous over-insurance, and a stern resolve to do no less than is necessary to those who fear a premature relaxation in the face of détente. There seems no doubt that the strategic nuclear forces necessary to maintain a deterrent balance will be kept up with or without SALT. Some sense of confidence at that level is the necessary precondition for a degree of complacency elsewhere. But whatever the theories of the present Administration, the pressures on general-purpose forces and hence the American conventional contribution to NATO will continue.

These pressures may perhaps be divided into two categories. On the one hand are the political pressures symbolised by the Mansfield Resolution; on the other hand are the resource-allocation dilemmas faced by a goverment with a limited budget in a period of severe domestic demands and of rapidly rising military costs. Both come together in the demand that the Europeans should do more in their own defence. In the short run the Administration can probably resist the political pressure for cuts in American contributions to European defence, though the electoral results of 1972 did nothing to strengthen the Administration's hand in Congress. In the somewhat longer run however – say four to six years – the budgetary pressures are likely to demand a reduction in American force levels in Europe, whatever the political climate, short of an unlikely recrudescence of the Cold War.

Even if the American military budget can be sustained in real terms, the rising cost of equipment and above all of manpower will almost certainly require a reduction in strength. This will be all the more so if, as seems more than likely, the SALT agreements fail to reduce expenditure on the essential strategic nuclear weapons. It seems improbable that the armed forces can recruit sufficient Army divisions on a voluntary basis to maintain the 15 divisions on which retention of present force levels in Europe is predicated. Pressure on the military budget will be aggravated if political irritation with Europe grows, and this might very well be the case as a result of commercial and monetary friction between the United States and the enlarged E.E.C.

For a variety of reasons, therefore, the prospect is for a reduced level of American military presence in Europe. This widely appreciated possibility has two distinguishable potential effects. In itself it may reduce the military effectiveness of NATO strategy. Secondly, it may erode the credibility of the American nuclear guarantee which is in any case being eroded by the growing recognition of mutual vulnerability. Neither possibility is inevitable or close to full realisation, but the two tendencies undoubtedly exist and constitute the essence of the present dilemma in American–European military relations.

The general mood of indifference to strategic matters in the present climate of détente forces one to ask, however, whether the dilemma is a serious one. Is there indeed any threat to European security and independence about which the Europeans need exercise themselves? If there is not, then there is presumably even less reason for the United States to be concerned. Indeed, the American perception of European complacency about the threat is a major source of support for the American advocates of a reduced United States military presence in Europe.

Few Europeans or Americans would rate the present danger of an overt Soviet military attack on Europe very high. The risks of such an adventure for the Soviet Union remain very great and it is difficult to see any incentive for the Russians to undertake such a gamble. But while this confident judgement is almost certainly justified under present circumstances, we must not forget that it is made within the context of a relatively high level of Western defensive efforts and diplomatic solidarity. The image of Soviet caution implied by the Western sense of reassurance is based very largely on the record of Soviet conduct when faced by such a strategic equilibrium. Thus we cannot rule out the possibility that a change in the military balance might promote a corresponding change in Soviet behaviour or, more plausibly, open the way for different Soviet responses in future political crises.

Much the same could be said of the more widely accepted anxiety that the danger posed for Europe by an erosion of Western defences lies in the direction of 'Finlandisation'. This concept, which seems to have been given a name by Professor Richard Lowenthal, consists of the gradual development of habits of enforced subservience to Russian preferences in both the foreign and domestic politics of ostensibly independent states. Those who are sceptical of any such danger point with some justification to the difficulty of specifying how the Soviet Union would translate its military predominance into political hegemony if it were unwilling – as the model implies – to launch actual aggression. Once again, however, we must remember that such backbone as West European governments have displayed has been stiffend by a fair semblance of military balance and an active American partnership. In the progressive climate of détente, few would rate the chances of a Soviet attack on Finland itself very likely, yet in détente the Finns appear no less subservient to their larger neighbour and even perhaps, a little more eager to undertake Russian diplomatic errands. Moreover, members of NATO themselves already show sensitivity to Soviet preferences, as some features of German *Ostpolitik* demonstrate. Perhaps the most apt forewarnings of the type of behaviour that can occur are provided by the anxiety of the Scandinavian members of NATO to avoid provocative military gestures in the face of the extending Soviet naval presence in Northern waters.

Considerations of this kind add up to a formidable case for believing that dismantling the Western structure of defence would involve an unwarranted venture into the unknown, entailing substantial risks for European independence. There has been a tendency in some European quarters to suggest that the E.E.C. might enjoy the experience of being a 'civilianised' power, typical of a new post-military age, and wielding political influence derived from economic weight. To some extent Japan is seen as a prototype for such a role. The analogy ignores, however the extent to which Japan has relied even more than Europe on the American umbrella and to which the prospective contraction of American power has prompted a rise in Japanese military pretensions. Moreover, a formula by which Europe pursues economic goals and ignores military requirements is certainly one calculated to accelerate the withdrawal of American power, for it would exacerbate all the American resentment at the inequitable incidence of military burdens. An early glimpse of the frictions possible is to be seen in the emergence of E.E.C. policy in the Mediterranean, which strikes many Americans as a division of responsibilties in which the United States has the Sixth Fleet and Europe has the trade. Finally, a civilianised concept of indifference to military concerns tends to ignore the possible occasions for spontaneous conflict which still exist in Europe, notably in Eastern Europe and the Balkans. Given the proven Soviet propensity to use military force to handle episodes on the periphery of their bloc, it requires considerable optimism to believe that steady West European nerves could survive the radical decay of the alliance and its defences before a European equivalent has been created.

If one adheres to the belief that for these reasons it is essential to preserve a framework of defence involving a significant American role, it remains to consider what the minimal requirements are. It seems clear that the flexible response is merely a reasonably elastic tripwire. The basis of West European security against Russian aggression is nuclear deterrence. This deterrence arises from the residual credibility of American strategic nuclear action, complicated by the existence of the European strategic nuclear forces. Small though the latter are, no one with any real appreciation of nuclear weapons can suppose the Anglo-French forces to be a negligible factor in Soviet calculations. The future development of those forces is therefore a central issue for the evaluation of European security, though not one that can be adequately discussed here. It is an issue that cannot be swept under the carpet much longer, both because some practical decisions have to be made by the European nuclear powers about the future of this hardware, and because SALT cannot proceed much further without a sequel to the earlier Soviet effort to introduce the European forces into the strategic calculation.

But although deterrence is the essence of European security, the flexible response cannot be dismissed as no more than a tripwire in the crude and simple sense. A certain level of conventional force is required to deal with minor incidents if they occur. More important, a degree of flexibility, and some kind of cushioning 'pause', is the necessary condition for the issue of the American strategic guarantee. A stark and immediate prospect of escalation to strategic nuclear action has been unacceptable to American expert opinion as an overt policy ever since the end of the Eisenhower Administration. The change in strategic conditions and in the American outlook could, however, give this long-established factor a new significance, for while hitherto the need to avoid nuclear annihilation on behalf of Europe posed a difficult strategic problem for the United States, the problem could, of course, be solved at a stroke if Americans decided to withdraw their guarantee. At a time when SALT symbolises American anxiety to avoid strategic nuclear actions and trends in force levels are eroding local defences, Europeans need to be very wary of any behaviour that gives undue prominence to the strategic nuclear risks at the heart of the North Atlantic alliance. If only for this reason, the European members of NATO need to possess at least a semblance of local defence that can make the risks run by the United States appear manageable, and this semblance needs to be proof against periods of renewed tension and not merely something that can be swallowed at a time of euphoric détente.

The prospect that no number of Cassandra-like warnings will wholly arrest the rundown of conventional forces at the disposal of the alliance has led to searches for new strategies. These searches are based on the assumption that increased divisional frontages, inferior logistics and shortage of heavy weapons will, whatever the outcome of mutual balanced force reductions (M.B.F.R.), make the existing strategy of maintaining a continuous, forward defence of traditional type impracticable and, perhaps more important, deprive it of credibility as a goal for military training.

There are therefore two interlocked problems for NATO today. One is to devise a strategy compatible with reduced forced levels; the other is to retain American participation in that strategy. Obviously success in solving one problem is a prime condition for success with the other. No strategy will be of much use if it does not involve the United States, but the Americans are unlikely to maintain their part if no plausible framework for military action short of nuclear holocaust exists. Several different though related approaches to this problem are being pursued, either in actual policy or in strategic speculation.

One escape from NATO's dilemmas would be to reduce the threat. While this goal is sought in vague political terms under the rubric of détente, in military form it underlies the concept of M.B.F.R. M.B.F.R., however, is unlikely to do more than palliate NATO's deficiencies; there is no reason to believe that such asymmetric limitations can be foisted on to the Soviet Union that the likely rundown of NATO forces will be fully offset.

Another solution is seen, especially by Americans, in the concept of burden-sharing. The wide variations in the defensive efforts of the individual European nations, when expressed in the aggregate, as they so often are in the United States, delude many Americans into believing that the major European nations contribute far less to the common effort than is in fact the case. There is also great confusion between the absolute economic burden and the balance-of-payments effect of American contributions to European defence. But whatever the merits of the case, there can be no doubt that a greater appearance of European effort is probably essential if even the best-disposed American administrations are to curb the indigenous pressures for a reduction in American support for NATO. Moreover it is, of course, obvious that any increase in European efforts would do something to ease the practical military as well as the transatlantic diplomatic problems of NATO. In the early 1970s most, though not all, of the West European nations made a better attempt to respond to the burden-sharing imperative than many observers would have cared to predict at the beginning of the Nixon Administration. While it is true that the alleged extra efforts contained a good deal of window-dressing and often disguised the effects of inflation as an increase in real expenditure, the spirit was the right one and at least the trend was not precipitately downwards. The days when the Europeans believed that greater efforts on their part would merely encourage the United States to do less seem to be definitely over.

None the less, there are a few who believe that the combined effect of apparent détente, domestic demands on the budget, and the rising costs of military equipment and manpower, will not reduce NATO force levels over the medium term and do so more rapidly than any parallel tendency on the Soviet side. Interest therefore continues in new strategies to maintain a semblance of conventional, forward, defence – adjectives necessary to preserve the morale of Americans and Germans respectively, and of others according to their strategic philosophy and geographical location. The most favoured and theoretically interesting schemes have been those for a concept of barrier defence which are discussed briefly elsewhere in this volume. Such a concept involves the employment of reserve and militia units exploiting cheap modern anti-armour and anti-aircraft weapons to establish a forward delaying barrier, while preserving the virtues of mobile defence for a core of highly equipped armoured and air cavalry units. Something of this kind has much to recommend it as the best way to exploit limited forces in delaying actions and has the merit of responding to many of the political constraints at work within the allied countries. Nevertheless, the idea has yet to survive the ordeal of sustained analysis, let alone experience.

To many advocates of a conventional barrier defence, not the least of its virtues is postponement or even total abandonment of tactical nuclear action. There is another school of thought, small but persistent, that believes it is precisely in the direction of tactical nuclear weapons that the answer to NATO's problems lies. In its most recent incarnation, this school emphasises the virtues of new miniature nuclear

weapons which can afford heavy firepower by comparison
with conventional weapons yet would allegedly permit the
limitation of collateral damage and the preservation of control and an orderly battlefield. The technical elements making
such employment practicable are chiefly nuclear plenty, com-
pact weapons, and improved accuracy and fusing. Pre-
positioned atomic demolition weapons would, of course,
provide perfect accuracy.

The opposition to such a strategy arises chiefly from those
who accept the 'firebreak' argument, believing that once any
nuclear weapons are used, escalation to catastrophic levels of
employment would be highly probable if not inevitable. Study
of Soviet tactical nuclear doctrine and of the Soviet stockpile
suggests that in a nuclear battle the Soviet forces would proceed to extremes wholly incompatible with the restrained,
quasi-conventional employment envisaged by the new school
of advocates for tactical nuclear weapons on the Western
side. Moreover, there is considerable force in the argument
that if the Soviet Union is intent on any serious offensive
actions, its strategic doctrine calls for large-scale nuclear
action from the start.

Certainly, it seems very unlikely that the 'conventionalised'
tactical nuclear option will win any quick ascendancy over
NATO doctrine. Yet the advocates of the strategy have their
finger on a critical flaw in NATO's present posture which the
combination of SALT and M.B.F.R. will progressively illu-
minate. For NATO's strategy already calls for the first use
of nuclear weapons in ways that lead even more directly to
escalation, and this strategy opens up the basic divergence
between American and European – especially continental
European and German – interests. While it is in the interest
of the United States to ensure that a tactical nuclear engagement remains below the strategic threshold as long as possible, to offer a chance of defence or negotiation short of
annihilation, for the Europeans a prolonged tactical nuclear
war with current doctrines and stockpiles is already annihilation. This divergence of interest underlies the confusion of
NATO nuclear doctrine, within which a limited and sketchy
agreement has been reached on guidelines for initial use of
nuclear weapons and little or no consensus exists as to 'follow-

on' use. Moreover, many practical military men have little faith in the technical efficacy of the procedures and doctrines that do exist.

President Nixon's quest for further options, one expression of which was quoted above, indicates a healthy recognition of this problem. Whether the consequence of this recognition is healthy for the American contribution to defence and deterrence in Europe depends on the answers that he finds. In this context, the underlying meaning of the argument for a more limited tactical nuclear strategy becomes clearer. The present posture, with a brief conventional pause leading to tactical nuclear weapons that have ranges of hundreds of miles and yields of up to 400–500 kilotons, merges the tactical response imperceptibly into the strategic strike when the chief enemy is geographically contiguous to the battle zone. This the Soviet Union clearly recognised by its efforts to have the forward-based systems included in the SALT calculations.

A move towards revising the NATO tactical nuclear stockpile and doctrine of use so as to reinforce the distinction between battlefield and strategic use may therefore become a condition of retaining American participation in a defence that is less than adequate in conventional terms and must therefore contain a nuclear element. Such a shift would naturally arouse some European misgivings, for the divergence of American and European interests would not disappear by magic. Any reassurance to the United States about the dangers of escalation can be purchased only at the price of some European anxiety that the deterrent against aggression has been eroded. One's judgement of the benefits or dangers of such a move would be greatly conditioned by one's estimate of how far the defensive potential of NATO had been increased and by one's willingness to rely instead on the continued deterrent effect of an American promise of strategic nuclear action on Europe's behalf – a promise that, however incredible, could scarcely be wholly discounted by the Soviet Union. This kind of residual reassurance is at its weakest when the possibility of some spontaneous outbreak of hostilities in Europe is envisaged, for then Soviet conduct would be derived from events rather than prior calculation.

The more the actual use of tactical nuclear weapons as a means of defence rather than a tool of deterrence is considered, the more the Europeans will wish to have their own control over how far the conflict may go before the superpowers cease to be immune. This need already exists within presently approved NATO strategy, and such reassurance as the Europeans possess lies in the Anglo-French strategic forces. The more these are introduced into the equation, the more uneasy the United States may become, but it is worth considering whether this uneasiness would be smaller rather than greater if the American contribution to tactical nuclear action were more sharply distinguished from the American strategic strike forces than is at present the case. One would thus end up with an equation whereby American strategic forces would deter a Soviet strike against the United States, European national forces would deter the Soviet M.R.B.M.s and set limits on other Soviet theatre nuclear forces, while small, unmistakably tactical, battlefield, nuclear weapons would stiffen the conventional defence. We must recognise, however, something that the advocates of the small nuclear weapons often omit from their argument: that if the small weapons are to do much to reduce American anxieties about the risk inherent in the NATO commitment, they must do so by making an effective defence more possible, not by merely introducing a brief extra step in the process of escalation. The attractions of a mini-nuclear strategy therefore depend very much on the military efficacy of such weapons in improving the capability of the defensive combatant. This efficacy remains as unproven as the validity of the conventional barrier concept.

Given all the intellectual difficulties and divergences of interest as well as opinion, it is unlikely that NATO will move rapidly towards any formal or overt revision of strategy. But it is towards some combination of the conventional and tactical nuclear postures discussed here that the domestic and international pressures bearing on the individual members of the alliance are likely to drive the real capabilities of NATO. In particular it seems probable that the clearer definition of some intra-nuclear as well as pre-nuclear firebreak will be the necessary condition for the continued participation of the

United States in a tactical nuclear strategy for the defence of Europe.

There is, of course, a certain air of unreality about all discussions of strategy for the last resort in the nuclear age, and this is particularly so at a time of détente. The margins of deterrence are such that we can probably afford a degree of imprecision. The logic of Western policy may drift in the directions we have been discussing, but in practice the declared policies of NATO and the United States will probably continue to paper over the imperfect match of transatlantic interests with an agreed ambiguity. Unless we are most unfortunate, this very uncertainty will be sufficient to perpetuate military caution in Europe.

Such a situation is, however, uncomfortably vulnerable to sharp and unexpected changes in the character of either American or Soviet policy.

Burden-sharing may be an adequate slogan for today, but the recent evolution of world events in general and American policy in particular reinforces the case for believing that Europe must look more to its own security. The long years in which the United States has been the ultimate source of security and consequently the residual home of strategic responsibility has encouraged many Europeans to believe – often subconsciously and all the more effectively for that – that defence is an optional matter rather than a constant imperative. Those who optimistically espouse the idea that a 'civilianised' Europe can be prosperous, independent and secure, represent the logical culmination of this trend of thought. If they are right, all is well. If they are not, it will be no easy task to coax the Europeans to undertake the gradual construction of an adequate independent basis of security at a time when the overall political atmosphere is one of détente. To those who are not convinced 'civilianisers', however, the European balance of power is the condition for, not an alternative to, the relaxation of tension.

2
Future Relations between the United States and Europe

WAYNE WILCOX*

I. *A Changed World*

After twenty-five years of quite unusual strategic stability, the security relationships among the major world powers are returning to their historic natural state – flux. This has been painfully obvious to Soviet decision-makers concerned with their Chinese ex-ally, and equally clear if not so dramatic with their East European client-subjects.[1] The flux is also to be seen in the relationship between the United States and its NATO and Japanese allies. Since the beginning of the 1970s, change has accelerated and there is little reason to expect it to moderate because of some benign and intrinsic equilibrium process at work in world politics.

Much of the change in the American alliance systems was sought by Washington, but the emerging patterns represent major problems for American adversaries, allies, and its own foreign policy-making community. But it is also true that the world was changing dramatically below the veneer of the 'central strategic balance' between the two super-powers, and the alliance systems were themselves being transformed in the context of global change.

* Professor of Government, and Research Member of the Institute of War and Peace Studies, Columbia University, New York, presently on leave as Cultural Attaché, U.S. Embassy, London. The views presented in this paper are solely those of the author in his personal capacity.
[1] For an interesting analysis, see Robin Remington, *The Warsaw Pact: Case Studies in Communist Conflict Resolution* (Cambridge, Mass.: M.I.T. Press, 1971).

Conflict between states after 1945 proceeded by different means, at different scales and in different theatres with new or refurbished techniques. As Stanley Hoffman has quite correctly written, 'Nuclear weapons have not abolished war, they have displaced it.'[2] Massively asymmetrical military relationships in the nuclear age have not, as a consequence, had a high political 'output coefficient' for the great powers, although they have set boundaries to certain kinds of competition. Conflicts outside the core of the super-power central balance have continued in a historic way in many cases, but subject always to super-power 'trumping' through escalation of the resources committed in a struggle. Alliance systems during this period, however, provided an organisational structure for an increasing load of transaction involved in international interchange. In these, super-power *modus operandi* became a crucial factor in an emerging post-European world system.

These several developments have coincided with a transportation-communication revolution that has allowed and has been accompanied by the globalisation of foreign policy 'working space' for the great powers and much higher levels of segmentary social-economic integration between states. The result is an immensely complex tangle of international relations that makes the Cold War era, in retrospect, a model of relatively simple if unpleasant adversarial *Realpolitik*.

The American response to this much-changed and increasingly complex world, and to its position in that world, has been to look for ways and means to reduce costs, simplify foreign affairs management and balance the growing relative power of its strategic adversaries. This response is the consequence of many factors, principally a shift in national self-appraisal. As George Ball has rather sourly argued, widespread popular support for a burdensome set of foreign policy commitments was sure to weaken with

The advent of a postwar generation with little recollection of Stalinist years, the loss of authority and self-confidence of the United States as a result of the Vietnamese embroglio, the acceptance of parity in nuclear weapons which has

2 'Weighing the Balance of Power', *Foreign Affairs*, L, 4 (July 1972), 625.

diminished the credibility of the American deterrent and the normal desire of people to achieve that state of grace which is vaguely thought of as normality. . . .[3]

While foreign policy managers looked for relevant priorities and to a simplified strategic posture,[4] and while publics looked *to* their domestic problems and *for* Mr Ball's 'state of grace' – 'Come Home America', the McGovern slogan of 1972 – Congressional leaders looked for ways to save public money. It was not only Senator Mike Mansfield who noted that in 1949 the United States and its Western allies were spending 5 per cent of their G.N.P.s on defence; Twenty years later America was spending about 10 per cent and its NATO allies 4 per cent. Japan, the other 'rich' ally, was spending less than 1 per cent. Moreover, some major allies made clear a declining actual commitment to alliance missions in favour of national interests, whether at policy autonomy or of defence industry procurement politics. Many Congressional leaders argued for reduced United States commitments to the defence of prosperous nations who, they believed, asked of America financial sacrifices in excess of those they asked of their own peoples. Moreover, United States NATO expenditures were seen as significant factors in America's adverse balance of payments after 1971.

Another factor in the American self-appraisal is harder to weigh in its consequences. Beginning in the early 1960s, after the 'spirit of Camp David' and the development of the Soviet–American dialogue, many American analysts concluded that the Cold War was perhaps as much exacerbated by the United States as stimulated by the actions of the Soviet Union. The so-called revisionist historians and 'New Left' polemicists were but the tip of an iceberg; détente somehow seemed both overdue and 'safe' to a broad segment of the informed public. Arms control became as valid a goal as arms superiority; a negotiated strategic relationship with Moscow became, somehow, a not altogether Utopian notion. Even

---

[3] Testimony before the Subcommittee on NATO Commitments, Armed Services Committee, House of Representatives, 24 Feb 1972.

[4] An early example of this approach is Henry A. Kissinger, *The Troubled Partnership: A Reappraisal of the Atlantic Alliance* (New York: McGraw-Hill, for the Council on Foreign Relations, 1965).

sceptics admitted that one might as well claim virtue of what was painful necessity – mutual super-power deterrence ruled out effective United States coercive nuclear diplomacy after about 1964. And this important realisation called into question the efficacy of the United States 'umbrella' for allies, especially in the absence of a viable United States 'damage limitation' capability relevant to limited nuclear war. *Both* super-powers had the ability to raise all conflicts between them to the central war level.

Coupled with these developments were three crucial problems/opportunities of the early 1970s. The first, crucial in adversarial diplomacy, was the radical deterioration of relations between Russia and China, and China's willingness to involve Washington in the quarrel. This allowed America to begin to lower the United States military posture in most of Asia – the Nixon Doctrine – and, equally importantly, to develop a new counter in its relations with the Soviet Union. Of necessity, this quite dramatic if obvious shift (made the more noteworthy because of the unique nature of diplomacy in democratic states with regularly scheduled elections) left both Japan and India discomfited.

The second area of problems/opportunities was caused by the dollar crisis and the related international economic negotiations necessary to undergird world trade. While experts have disagreed on what would have been the best American response,[5] the Administration felt impelled to act dramatically, and essentially unilaterally. This policy, and former Treasury Secretary Connally's presentation of it in subsequent negotiations, left America's allies with policies which they found politically sensitive and/or economically difficult.

The third area of choice was super-power 'bilateralism': agreements essentially worked out in Moscow and Washington and communicated to the world. America's allies welcomed a measured relaxation of tension, but were concerned that the process by which it was arranged might leave them isolated and uninfluential.

In sum, the American role in world strategic relationships

[5] See C. Fred Bergsten's 'The New Economics and U.S. Foreign Policy', *Foreign Affairs*, L, 2 (Jan 1972) 199–222, for a review.

and in international economics remains crucial but has become more uncertain. Europeans and Japanese find their security and preferred form of international organisation almost wholly dependent upon the American commitment to it, yet they lack assured responses or even a sense of viable access to decision points within Washington. Moreover, American society appears to be so mercurial and social change so rampant that few governments have confidence in their ability to forecast future United States policies. Specifically, allied governments might reasonably wonder whether any President would be willing to define as a 'vital' interest a sub-nuclear conflict involving an American ally[6] and the Soviet Union or China, or, if he was so willing, whether the Congress, public opinion and a volunteer army would permit the honouring of his commitments.

It is therefore not difficult to share with Alastair Buchan the view that 'It is difficult to believe that the 1970s can pass without a radical reorganisation of the structure and probably the strategy of NATO'.[7] While this has been said, more or less consistently, since the early 1960s,[8] most of the past analyses concerned variables other than major shifts in United States policy. A fruitful look at European security in the 1970s must begin with the Atlantic variable in a newly changed world.

II. *The Matter of Primacy*

American diplomacy must now reconcile the national interest, the adversaries' vital interests and allied vital interests. The 'mix' of possible policies ranges from isolationism, through super-power bilateralism to a tight collective-security diplomacy. In the nature of international politics no major power can pursue a wholly 'pure' category of diplomacy, but neither

[6] This problem is certainly more severe for Third World countries outside alliance systems, such as India, and forfeit to super-power 'balancing' interests that ignore their unique problems.

[7] 'A World Restored?', *Foreign Affairs*, L, 4 (July 1972) 650.

[8] Of the many examples, perhaps three might suffice as exemplary: Klaus Knorr (ed.), *NATO and American Security* (Princeton Univ. Press, 1959); Helmut Schmidt, *Defence or Retaliation: A German View* (New York: Praeger, 1962); and W. T. R. Fox and Annette B. Fox, *NATO and the Range of American Choice* (New York: Columbia Univ. Press, 1967).

can the national, adversary and allied interests be easily reconciled, especially in such an important area as Europe. The problems of the Third World demonstrate how even more complex their reconciliation can be in the light of these varying diplomatic imperatives in more 'vital' areas.

At the centre of American concern is the strategic balance between the United States and the Soviet Union. This relationship is 'maximum risk', 'maximum cost', and the nature of weapons technology ensures that it will remain so for the foreseeable future. Super-power relations, whether of détente or conflict, are of the greatest politico-military priority. American goals in other sectors of diplomacy must serve 'deterrence'. This is the core of the central balance, but covers but a small band of the spectrum of relations between Washington and Moscow in the world. As one moves away from the United States – Soviet Union central war contingency, deterrence diplomacy becomes less relevant and certainly less clear. By the time one considers Third World contingencies, central balance considerations are clearly peripheral.

The problem for Europe and Japan is that they are not directly principal parties to the 'core' deterrent relationship, and are uncertain, in varying degrees, of their place in super-power 'skirmish rules'. They lie hostage to miscalculated strategic balances, and to collusive agreements between the super-powers. They lack a 'trigger' for the American gun, or a gun of their own of adequate military calibre. Japan has the additional problem of the Chinese 'super-state'.

In the case of NATO, and Japan, the United States has firm and explicit treaty commitments to defend its allies should they be directly attacked. Most Europeans accept that commitment as one that would be honoured, and certainly all American decision-makers are on record as continuing to support collective-security diplomacy. The stationing of large numbers of American troops in Europe and to a lesser degree Japan makes an attack on allied countries an attack on the United States in any case. The degree to which a crude 'hostage' theory of collective response is more credible than a sophisticated legal/national interest theory lies at the heart of the problem of United States troop reductions or withdrawals during a period of super-power bilateralism. In his 1972 'State of the World' address to Congress, however, President Nixon argued for larger NATO conventional forces precisely because 'American forces should not be reduced to the role of a hostage, triggering automatic use of nuclear weapons at the very time when the strategic equation makes such a strategy less plausible'.

The operational problem is that the Soviet Union would be unlikely directly and unambiguously to threaten NATO, an action that would surely galvanise America with a 'Pearl Harbour' effect. If Moscow did so, it would represent such a dangerous deviation of Soviet policy that the United States would be forced to respond in any case. The more likely contingencies lie in a range of more ambiguous coercive bargaining situations in which the Soviet Union would exert influence by means short of armed intervention, but under conditions in which the threatened state would find it 'cost-effective' to accommodate Soviet interests. The possible resultant pattern is often labelled 'Finlandisation'.

This pattern of increasing Soviet influence short of direct intervention could take place in the absence of countervailing American power, in the event of disunity within the NATO alliance[9] or if coalition governments in Western states found the price of governance to be closer co-operation with Soviet patrons of domestic parties. An attractive combination of concessional trade/resource transfers and reduced antagonisms might make the political costs of this transition low, especially if supportive public opinion had been created in an era of super-power détente and troubled United States – European trade or alliance relations.

While these possibilities are increasingly understood in the United States, both the national interest and the United States–Soviet relationship argue for bilaterally negotiated super-power reductions in force in strategic weapons and in European deployments, basing and posture. Arms-control agreements in nuclear weapons are the easiest area for accord; they can be negotiated without fundamentally affecting

[9] Christoph Bertram has made this exceedingly clear in his closely argued *Mutual Force Reductions in Europe: The Political Aspects*, Adelphi Paper No. 84 (London: International Institute for Strategic Studies, 1972).

either the relative strengths of the parties in the central balance, or their power vis-à-vis the rest of the world.[10] In the sense that such agreements symbolise the end of American nuclear hegemony, they weaken the 'deterrence by loan' assumptions of some governments, but in any case they reflect a new military reality and do not by themselves change strategic relationships.

Arms-control agreements outside the nuclear weapons 'central balance' area are much more complex, because they require trade-offs between allied concerns and Soviet concerns. The Nixon visit to the Soviet Union led to the announcement of three openings for discussion and possible accommodation: European postures and force levels, further strategic reductions in SALT II, and possible third area 'rules of restraint'. If agreement could be reached in any of these areas, it would represent a structural change in United States –Soviet relationships. For that reason, America's allies are most concerned about the possibility that agreement would be 'purchased' at their expense. More precisely, they are apprehensive that United States détente diplomacy, whether motivated by domestic pressures or strategic calculus, would result in agreements which would limit European and/or Japanese choices in areas of importance to them.

This question is often put grossly; does the United States value an improvement in relations with the Soviet Union more than the maintenance of stable, good, treaty relationships with its NATO allies? It is an easy 'no', generally officially stated as: 'The security of the United States is linked directly to the security of Western Europe, a centre of technological and economic power second only to our own. We have a vital interest in deterring Soviet efforts to impose their will on Western Europe through military or political means.'[11] But the question is poorly put. The real issue is differing notions of how far the United States can go in developing better relations with the Soviet Union without com-

[10] This has led to a jaundiced view of arms control 'successes' by many analysts, especially those from middle powers. See, for example, Alva Myrdal, 'The Game of Disarmament', *Impact* (Paris: UNESCO, Summer 1972).

[11] 'Europe: U.S. Forces', Dept. of State, Bureau of Public Affairs, *GIST*, 17(rev.2) (Apr 1972).

promising the fundamental interests of NATO allies, and at what cost the United States will continue to support stable treaty relationships with NATO partners.

Current American declaratory policy calls for the maintenance of present, costly, commitment levels at least as long as SALT, *Ostpolitik* and further Russo-American discussions are in progress. That these are related is explicitly acknowledged in official publications justifying NATO commitment levels on the grounds, *inter alia*, that a cut would 'raise European concern that we might disregard allied interests in order to reach agreement with the Soviets. This is a particularly serious concern at a time when strategic arms limitation talks are under way between the U.S. and the U.S.S.R.'[12]

If however a European security conference or success in the mutual balanced force reduction (M.B.F.R.) diplomacy resulted in an agreement on lowered conventional force levels in Europe, Washington might press to make the reductions 'stationed troops'. This would be desirable as a reciprocal United States–Soviet action in Europe, and would both reduce United States costs and provide more manageable force levels for a volunteer American Army. Of the 310,000 United States personnel assigned to NATO, 215,000 are in Germany and 195,000 are Army troops. 'Central Theatre' reductions therefore look quite attractive if they can be attained without significantly undermining the military security of various NATO countries, notably Germany

To a degree the answers to these questions lie in the future and are subject to a series of imponderable choices in the various capitals. Sooner or later, however, Europeans will have to 'weigh in', and with more than near-empty diplomatic statements, delivered *seriatim*.

If one assumes that the United States will continue to bargain with the adversary until the military costs are lowered appreciably, and that the Europeans will have to become partners in the bargaining by pledging more real resources if they disagree with a proposed bargain, the analyst is brought abrupty to the bar: what is European defence policy other than the American umbrella, suitably multicoloured? How much consensus exists among governments,

[12] Ibid.

and between governments and people, on defence postures relevant to NATO and the East? How much elasticity exists in public budgets for major new defence efforts? Is there, in fact, a European strategic reserve of sufficient flexibility that it could meet crises that may have a very short development phase?[13]

It seems to be clear that there is no single European view of *défense sans les Américains.* NATO doctrine shifts must be made in the light of their selective effects on the various countries. Tactical nuclear weapons launch and use doctrine, for example, is closely tied to German notions of the optimum battlefield.[14] The location of NATO North outside Oslo – itself now complicated by Norway's refusal to join the E.E.C. and strong pressure to quit NATO – and the various command locations elsewhere in the area stem from discrete interests and concerns with military posture. The preferred French posture of political alliance and military autonomy is perhaps the most obvious example of a generic problem.

Moreover, the European capitals, like Washington, have great difficulties justifying large defence budgets and standing military forces in a period sometimes characterised as one of 'détente'.[15] Both the French and the British are committed to large expenditures on strategic weapons systems, and the Germans appear to have more 'cash' than military manpower in meeting their NATO goals. The smaller countries of the alliance are relatively marginal contributors to overall defence posture in the alliance, and the Italians operate a 'NATO South' diplomacy that has much in common with a past attention paid to the Mediterranean.[16]

---

[13] The British position is summarised in 'Standing By: Britain's Strategic Reserve', *Economist*, 29 Apr 1972. The French case is put in the first French Defence White Paper, June 1972.

[14] Such doctrine is itself highly complex and rather unclear. See Victor Gilinsky, 'Arms Control Aspects of the Deployment of Tactical Nuclear Weapons in Europe', Southern California Arms Control and Foreign Policy Seminar (Oct 1971).

[15] See Josef Korbel's *Détente* (Princeton Univ. Press, 1972), for an elaboration and explication of the terms applied in this era.

[16] Moreover, Italian domestic politics is polarised in such a way that NATO commitment levels are seen as an indication of anti-Communist Party of Italy interests, rather than as European defence interests.

The over-arching problem, however, is one of scale. No European leader can imagine that his country, singly or in concert with other smaller European countries, can deter, let alone balance, the Soviet super-power. American strength must be invoked. If the Americans are invoked, European defence efforts are, to a degree, superfluous. A conventional Soviet attack on Western Europe, given the levels of man-power, equipment superiority and favourable terrain, would be successful, probably in a relatively short campaign, in the absence of massive American conventional or nuclear in-volvement. The British and French nuclear forces would be suicidal to invoke because of Soviet second-strike capabili-ties. Should such a case develop, it might be argued that the Europeans would realise that their societies are less resilient than in the past, that the level of destructiveness of such a war would be overwhelming, and that the future of Europe would, in any case, be settled 'over their heads'. In these circumstances, a prudent policy would be one of minimum defence expenditure, maximum exertions on behalf of a security alliance with the United States, and a 'low threshold' for United States military response to Soviet initiatives. That this is the practical obverse of the contemporary American interest is a paradox of the times (if not an altogether un-pleasant one for European treasury chiefs to contemplate). While it is cheap, however, it leaves the Europeans and the Japanese essentially vulnerable to an uncertain, distant and newly vulnerable country.

In operational terms, therefore, American reductions in force commitments to Europe are likely to produce even more marked European reductions in defence effort. This will maintain the strategic relationship with the alliance, which is keyed, for most European planners, on a 'low thres-hold' American entry. The greatest strength in such a rela-tionship is the appearance of imminent collapse on the part of the weak partner, by which it ensures an attentive posture on the part of the strong. There are two collateral dangers of this strategy; the first is that it will drive the United States (or it will be driven) to real isolationism, after which Europe will have no alternative to 'Finlandisation' and the second is that the low threshold will become defined as a low nuclear threshold, subject to the constraints of the central deterrent balance, and hence possibly subject to paralysis or high-risk instability.

The NATO military hedge against this contingency is a conventional force posture high enough to raise the 'opportunity costs' for Soviet coercive bargaining, and to allow the middle ground between local exchanges and central war to be ambiguous – 'flexible response' expressing the ambiguity between 'defence' and 'deterrence'. The optimum diplomatic hedge is widespread 'normalisation' between Western and Eastern Europe.

It seems clear that both ends of the division of labour in deterrence are covered: the United States covers central nuclear war contingencies and the European states cover low-intensity and local contingency Soviet probings. The European–American dialogue on burden-sharing concentrates on the cost of the middle-range defence contingencies of the flexible response doctrine. The problem lies in the fact that the total NATO country contingents in Germany (the United Kingdom, France, Belgium, Canada and the Netherlands) number 143,000, less than half of the American NATO force commitment of the United States. Moreover, the United States contributes all the tactical nuclear forces of NATO, and manages the security, storage and battleworthiness of the some 7,000 nuclear warheads in the NATO inventory. In both the Mediterranean and the North Sea, United States naval forces are the heart of the maritime defence of Europe.

It is this imbalance of 'middle ground' contingency risks and costs which most concerns American planners and which is most difficult for both the European and the American governments to explain and justify to their parliaments. The middle-ground contingencies in fact cover the special interests, and the separate interests, of the various European NATO countries. They are politically salient even if militarily less probable than contingencies on either end of the deterrence scale. *They represent, therefore, the prime military costs of a political relationship.* It is not unnatural that the United States believes that this cost should be borne much more equitably, nor unnatural that the European NATO countries should believe that this is a matter for the large partner to bear 'in the interests of the alliance'.

This intra-alliance bargaining 'choreography' has become almost classical in NATO discussions. Since it has proven politically counter-productive and, Germany aside, militarily only partially rewarding to push for burden-sharing, the United States naturally believes that a sound strategy is to pursue negotiations with the adversary to lower the entire counter-force cost of the United States–European NATO posture. If 'stationed troops' would allow both the Soviet Union and the United States to conduct a parsimonious withdrawal of some divisions, the United States NATO 'burden' would be less and the alliance would have fewer bargaining strains. The recurrent difficulty of this strategy is that the Europeans believe the United States might negotiate away their interests and redelne 'flexible response' in ways that made the lower end of the deterent–defence spectrum much more burdensome for them. They could then resolve this problem only by political accommodation with the East.

The essential NATO operating code was fashioned in the years of American military and economic supremacy. As reconstruction proceeded and the European Common Market provided the confidence and structure for rapid economic growth, the American economy was shifting to an unprecedented 'post-industrial' service-sector-dominant economy. Because the North American continent is rich in raw materials and because the 1960s found the United States with high research-and-development products and processes to market, the eroding real export performance of the restructured United States economy was masked.

In the mid-1960s three major trends took their toll of the 'almighty' dollar, at least on the short-term current account sheets. The first was the Vietnamese war and the very high level of external expenditures necessary to support it, including imports into the United States of consumer goods that would otherwise have been in short supply. This appreciably affected the balance-of-payments position, especially as the war in Vietnam in the late 1960s was costing $20-24 billion a year. The second factor rocking the dollar's role was the changing foreign investment pattern of United States business. Both as an offset to possible E.E.C. protectionism and in order to capture a fair share of European high-technology industry, American firms invested heavily abroad. These capital transfers, or remittances not sent home, or borrowings on the European capital markets – especially the Euro-dollar market – contributed to an ever strong long-term capital portfolio for United States businesses abroad, but at the cost of short-term foreign exchange balances.[17] The third factor weakening the dollar was continued high levels of official transfers for military and economic assistance. In 1970 the United States provided $680 million in military assistance and $2,910 million in economic transfers.[18]

These several developments, coupled with the long-range transformation of the nature of the American economy, spelled trouble for the role of the trading dollar, and for the international economic system which had come to depend upon the dollar as the instrument of liquidity in financing much higher levels of international trade. When the nonconvertible dollar was effectively devalued against gold, and European and Japanese currencies revalued against the dollar, the financial pressures on all official transfers of the United States were accentuated. This tended to put the cost of American forces in Europe – rich, revalued Europe – in the political limelight.

At about the same time, Europeans had become increasingly concerned about the American-based multinational corporations, and the 'foreign purchase' of major firms. Between 1960 and 1969 United States private longterm investments in Europe increased from $6.7 billion to $21.55 billion; in the E.E.C. countries from $2.6 billion to $10.2 billion.[19] American managers and management procedures brought *Le Défi Américain* to the best-seller lists in France and throughout Europe; American banks and bankers moved into the rich capital pool that the Euro-dollar and Euro-bond

[17] In 1970, U.S. assets abroad totalled $158 billion, and foreign assets in the United States totalled $90.8 billion, a surplus of $52.7 billion. American foreign investments showed an increase of $6 billion in 1971, the year the dollar was devalued. *Statistical Abstract of the United States, 1971* (Washington: Government Printing Office, 1971) p. xxiv.   [18] Ibid.

[19] *U.S. Statistical Abstract, 1971*, p. 755.

markets represented;[20] American-based multinational corporations, in a series of bold acquisition moves, turned autonomous corporations into branches, and United States
high-technology firms, such as I.B.M. all but smothered the
computer industry of Europe under its more efficient, advanced and skilful marketing and servicing procedures, at
least temporarily.

   The effect in Europe was unsettling, and it was not merely
de Gaulle's France that considered a defensive economic
nationalism that had implications for NATO alliance policy.
The effect in the United States was also unsettling. Jobs were
thought to have been 'exported', and nationally financed high
technology was widely diffused by United States firms
abroad. This appeared to deepen the foreign exchange problem in the short run, did nothing to reduce the unemployment percentages in the United States, and skewed the
benefits of American scientific investments in favour of
stockholders of the multinational corporation rather than the
American worker, locality or taxing authority. The problem
was illustrated by such curious situations as the Ford Motor
Company importing into the United States German-built
Fords (no doubt assembled by Italians, Greeks and Yugoslavs), thereby contributing to the glut of dollars in the
German treasury, the absence of new jobs in the American
automobile industry, the balance-of-payments difficulties of
the United States, but the handsome profit of multinational
Ford shareholders and managers. The collateral problems
were equally paradoxical: the Deutsches Bundesbank, in
order to get rid of dollars or secure high interest from their
investment, 'loaned' them to American banks via the Euro-
dollar and Euro-bond markets, thereby allowing American
firms to buy European enterprises with the selfsame dollars.
In the meantime, the German economy appeared to be over-
heated because of domestic purchasing power generated by
high activity, while the American economy was sluggish
because of unemployment, low levels of investment in new
plant and technology, and declining labour productivity
coupled with inflation as Americans attempted to buy 'cheap'

[20] See Stuart Robinson's new book tracing this development (The Hague,
1972).

foreign products. Small wonder that the dollar system col-
lapsed.

By 1972 the revalued pound had been floated downwards
and international monetary arrangements were both uncertain and tension-producing. The increasing interdependence
of the rich economies of Europe, Japan and North America
makes one society increasingly vulnerable to the problems
in another, and the key domestic indices of such problems –
unemployment and inflation – are at the heart of politics.[21]
Yet international economic semi-integration clearly diffuses
authority and autonomy. The effect has been a strengthening
of economic nationalism through government-blessed cartel-
isation on an all-Europe basis, and a tightening of government restrictions on foreign capital initiatives.

When these economic problems and structural characteristics are taken together with Europe's continued military
weakness and dependency upon the United States, and are
seen as part of the bargaining process within an alliance
which is itself part of a larger community of interests, even
the rather straightforward military-cost and equity arguments
of the 'simple problems' in NATO take on shadings and
variances of meaning that make effective negotiation and
change difficult. This is true not just between governments,
but within them as well.

The preponderant world role of the United States after the
Second World War was something of a historical accident.
The war galvanised and strengthened America while ravag-
ing most of the world's great powers. After the war, applied
science and technology transformed the American economy
in very productive ways, offering an already rich continent an
even greater temporary advantage over other rich states.
Nuclear weapons technology, itself an 'apex technology'
requiring almost all the skills a scientific nation can have, led
to the concentration and then the maintenance of immense
military force in a very few capitals, notably Washington.
Moreover, America was not war-weary and indeed had begun
to come out of its continental shell by 1945. Stalin's Russia,

---

[21] For a useful analysis, see Richard N. Cooper, *The Economics of Interdependence: Economic Policy in the Atlantic Community* (New York:
McGraw-Hill, for the Council on Foreign Relations, 1968).

aligned with Mao's Red China, gave democrats and nationalists no real alternative but close collaboration with the West's
new Rome. And like Rome, America rapidly became an imperial power with global interests and global responsibilities.

A generation after the Second World War, most of the
elements of the historical accident have changed. Most of
the world's great powers are back in centre stage, modestly
retitling themselves middle powers. Most of these states have
demonstrated that science and technology can do for a
resource-scarce society what it did for a resource-rich continent: witness Japan's miracle and Italy's remarkable growth
in the 1960s. Nuclear weapons technology is now within the
grasp of perhaps twenty-five countries, and the super-powers
have maintained their distinctive title more because of their
missile, command and control, and A.B.M. technologies than
their decisive or monopolistic technological edge in nuclear
science. Americans have become world-weary and dis-
heartened with the 'Crimeas' of Korea and Vietnam, and the
responsibilities without the glories of being leader of the
West's legions. Stalin's Russia is changed, having become a
more powerful if more conventional state with the passage of
time, and Mao's China appears increasingly able to make its
voice heard in the strategic discussions of the world.

These changes do not detract from America's great wealth,
power, military force or global presence, but they mean that
spent resources 'purchase' less because the scale of the process has increased so dramatically. Every increment of new
foreign influence is bought at an ever-greater cost, absolutely
and relatively, than in the past. This state of affairs coincides
with much-increased domestic demands on public funds, up
to this time available to an unusual degree for defence and
foreign affairs purposes.[22]

The sheer weight of domestic problems in a diverse continent experiencing great social change constitutes a non-
transferable burden for Washington. The newly enfranchised
ethnic minorities and newly visible social ills – poverty, health
care, narcotics, violence, urban decay, pollution – are trans-

[22] In part because very rapid economic growth in the 1950s and 1960s
gave American governments a growing 'pie' as well as a larger slice for
foreign affairs.

lated by the democratic process into much more urgent business than items on the agenda of foreign policy.

This is especially true in a period of more normal relations with the Soviet Union and China, the health of the developed countries, the general political stability of the Third World state order, and a strong belief in the remoteness of nuclear war. This kind of world was, after all, the goal of American diplomacy in the post-war period, and it is perhaps not unreasonable to expect American leaders to redirect their efforts to the home scene following its emergence.

An interdependent world in which economic health is multinational but military strength is still highly concentrated in two countries hardly allows for the United States to become 'isolationist', assuming its leaders or people wanted to do so. But that kind of world does allow for the less direct use of American power in the world, and a less interventionist diplomacy can therefore be quite as 'internationalist'. This would allow national interest to be satisfied within an alliance structure, but at a lower level of resource commitment.

It is difficult to imagine circumstances, short of imminent conflict in Europe, which would lead to greater American defence commitments in NATO. Such conflict appears to be highly unlikely over the next several years, and United States diplomacy is seeking to minimise even further the risks of such an eventuality.

It is equally difficult to imagine that the United States defence expenditure in Europe – perhaps $8 billion a year – will be immune from severe Congressional criticism. Past support for it from the armed services and the executive may also fade with a higher cost of new strategic weapons systems, a reduced defence budget and a smaller volunteer Army. It might, however, be argued that on all three counts the NATO alliance is cost-effective. Forward-based strategic systems may be less expensive (if more vulnerable than ICBMs), European contributions to NATO budgets may rise, and volunteers in the new Army may prefer Frankfurt, Germany to Frankfort, Kentucky.

A 'New European Defence Community'[23] seems unlikely

[23] See the article of that title by François Duchêne in *Foreign Affairs*, L, 1 (Oct 1971) 69–82.

in the absence of much greater unity in Europe than most expert observers believe to be probable. Nor is there any assurance that the E.E.C. of Nine will grow richer and more stable with every passing year, or that already low popular support for defence expenditures and Army service will increase. If present trends continue, and lower post-Northern Ireland British defence expenditures are assumed, there is every reason to believe that a lowered NATO posture, with or without major United States posture changes and with or without M.B.F.R., will emerge by 1975. To the degree that the Soviet Union maintains a retiring posture and the United States some measure of direct presence, this state of affairs might well be welcome in every Western capital.

The economic burdens of the alliance, *per se*, are manageable by the United States and, if their total scale is further reduced, should become much less of an irritant. The trade, currency and investment issues between the NATO countries are much more significant, if only for reasons of scale, depth of impact on politically sensitive areas of national life, and inherent difficulty. In future this set of problems will probably weigh more heavily with the Western Europeans and Japanese than with the United States, again principally because of scale but also because of the structure of the various trading economies.

The military paradox of the 1970s may turn out to be that an ever-richer Europe became more estranged from, and yet more dependent upon, the United States at precisely the time that the United States was reducing its direct commitments in NATO. This would almost surely lead to severe problems of mutual trust and co-operation, and questions about the future of the alliance would again shift from a focus on America to a set of foci in Europe.

What seems to be clear in any forecast is that for the 1970s, Europe – West and East – will remain at the centre of the interests of the super-powers. The nature of alliance and management policies may well shift to economics. As U. Alexis Johnson, Under-Secretary of State for Political Affairs, said to the U.S. House of Representatives Subcommittee on National Security Policy and Scientific

Development:[24] 'I expect that economic considerations may dominate foreign policy over the next two decades, as security concerns have dominated the last two.' Certainly, the 1972 'State of the World' address by President Nixon struck such a note in suggesting that

> So far, in practice, protection of certain special interests within Europe has been a major concern in the Community's collective decisions; this is the easiest course for an economic union that has yet to develop the political unity needed to make hard decisions taking account of interests outside the Community,[25]

and on troop costs in Europe:

> . . . we should work toward arrangements whereby the United States could maintain its forces in Europe with balance of payments consequences no different from those of maintaining the same forces in the United States. This would neutralise the balance of payments issue and allow the alliance to plan its forces on security criteria.[26]

It is difficult to be optimistic about these concerns over the near term. The expansion of the Europe of the Six to the Europe of the Nine, coupled with the expansion of E.E.C. trade preference zones, is unlikely to simplify the Community's structure or solidify its will to be generous in its dealings with a competitive United States, Japan or the Soviet Union. Nor are there many apparent trends in the capitals of its member states that would make greater defence agreements within NATO likely. Two problems from this prognosis seem inherent: greater tension within the politico-military blocs due to economic and social differences and competition based on such differences, and increasing levels of strategic and military accommodation between the super-powers because of the nuclear stalemate, growing military costs and decreasing political effectiveness of military diplomacy. Both these outcomes are likely to be much more pro-

---

[24] On 9 Aug 1972.
[25] 'U.S. Foreign Policy for the 1970s: The Emerging Structure of Peace', a report to the Congress by Richard Nixon, 9 Feb 1972, p. 18.
[26] Ibid., p. 20.

nounced in the West than in the East. As a result, détente in Europe will force the United States to develop a compensatory balance of power in Asia that will minimise Soviet opportunities for conventional military action in the West. This suggests a strengthening of United States ties with China, encouragement of Japanese defence efforts and collaboration with China, and an active Asian diplomacy in support of the maintenance of European détente and global peace. It also suggests that security concerns will continue to occupy Washington, both in the United States–Soviet context, and in Asia more generally, but that European problems may become economic in nature at the same time. In a sense, therefore, the 1970s are like the 1960s, except 'more of the same'.

3
Future Soviet Policy towards Western Europe

MALCOLM MACKINTOSH[*]

Any attempt to analyse Soviet policy towards Western Europe during the next decade must begin by looking at some of the fundamental factors which lie behind the Soviet Union's attitudes and outlook towards Europe. Certain assumptions must be made about Europe and about the Soviet Union, its government, and broad attitudes to international affairs during this period. Only when this has been done is it possible to draw some conclusions about Soviet policy towards Western Europe.

It is necessary, first of all, to recognise the status of the Soviet Union as a super-power, whose territory stretches right across the northern part of the Eurasian continent. It is at one and the same time a global power, the largest European power, a Far Eastern power, and the nearest super-power to the troubled areas of the Middle East. As seen from Moscow, Europe is the most important peninsula in the Eurasian continent; and the Russians have always been drawn to the idea that in any geographical grouping of states, the most powerful nation should naturally assume the leadership of the group. Therefore, in the most general terms, the Russians feel that Europe is part of 'their' continent, and that they have the right to be politically predominant in the European area. The presence of any other super-power, under whatever pretext, is regarded, in this broad sense, as an intrusion, to be eliminated if possible, without endangering the security of the Soviet Union.

[*] Consultant on Soviet Affairs to the International Institute for Strategic Studies, London.

Within this general framework, Europe is important to the Russians because of its geographical nearness to the heart of the Russian state, because it is the centre of that European civilisation to which Russians feel so strongly attracted, and because Western Europe succeeded in developing an economic, scientific and industrial strength which far outpaced anything which traditional Russia was able to achieve. Russia pushed westwards into the European peninsula partly in search of secure and viable frontiers, partly of outlets to ice-free ports, and partly in pursuit of this image of her rightful place in Europe. In doing so, Russia usually found that her advance was resisted, and on more than one occasion the countries of the European peninsula attempted to drive Russia out of Europe, and even overthrow the Russian state itself.

This long-drawn-out conflict and the destruction wrought on Russian soil (sometimes, as in the Second World War, far into the interior of the Russian heartland) have created a deep-seated fear in Russia of the power and resilience of the countries of the European peninsula, a fear which is fundamental to Soviet attitudes to Europe today. Indeed, this sense of fear is reinforced by the alliance of certain West European states with the other super-power, the United States, and the deployment of the latter's forces in Western Europe under the NATO alliance.

I believe that Soviet aims in Europe during the 1970s will probably still be formulated against the background of this long-standing Russian conviction that Europe should rightfully be part of their political sphere of interest. Their history has taught them that Europe as a whole does not accept this claim, and that attempts to pursue it by military means have caused Russia great suffering and loss. There is therefore likely to be a strong element of fear, suspicion and caution in Soviet approaches to European problems; but the possibility that any foreseeable Soviet Government will give up their basic long-term attitudes towards Europe is very remote.

If we are to speculate about Soviet policy in the 1970s, it is necessary to make a number of assumptions about both the Soviet Union and the international environment in which it has to operate. The first assumption, on which this paper is based, is that there will be no major military clash between

the Soviet Union and the West and that the Soviet Union will
retain its status and authority as a super-power with military
capabilities developing approximately along existing lines. It
is also assumed that no major war will take place between the
Soviet Union and China, but that the strains in the Sino-Soviet
relationship will be largely undiminished. Further assumptions implicit in the analysis are, first, that the existing European alliances, NATO and the Warsaw Pact, remain in being
with their present membership and broad capabilities, and,
second, that throughout the decade there will be a Soviet
regime composed of roughly the same type of Communist
leaders as today, operating as a collective leadership; and the
General Secretary of the Party is likely to remain as the
leader with the greatest authority.

On the subject of Soviet policies towards Western Europe,
perhaps the best way to tackle this is to recall Soviet attitudes
since the Second World War. At the end of the war, Stalin
believed that he had a chance to make considerable gains in
Europe, both territorially and through the establishment of
Communist regimes in a number of countries in the area,
largely by force or threat of force. His somewhat crude
attempts to extend his hegemony failed in Greece and Berlin,
and succeeded only in Czechoslovakia; within his own camp
Yugoslavia rebelled against his domination. After the failure
of the Berlin blockade in 1949, the Soviet Union, as it were,
'accepted' a kind of stalemate in Europe – and turned to the
Far East, where Mao Tse-tung had just taken power in China.
The 1949 stalemate, however, which I arbitrarily call 'Stalemate Mark I', was fundamentally a stalemate based on weakness. So that when the Soviet Union achieved super-power
status and reached rough strategic parity with the United
States – by the late 1960s – it was natural and characteristic that the Soviet leaders should seek ways of improving
upon it.

The first suggestion that the Soviet Union was thinking in
terms of some alteration to the political situation in Europe
came in 1967 at the time of the conference of ruling and non-
ruling Communist Parties held at Karlovy Vary in Czechoslovakia. Any plans which the Russians may have had,
however, in this direction had to be postponed because of the

distractions of the Middle East war of 1967 and the Czecho-slovak crisis of 1968. By late 1969, when the aftermath of the 'Prague Spring' had been dealt with, the Soviet Union returned to the theme of the future relationship of East and West in Europe. Soviet policy in Europe since 1969–70 has been preoccupied with preparing the stage for greater Soviet influence in, and weakening the cohesion of, Western Europe during the 1970s.

Let us look, then, at the situation of Europe as seen from Moscow which justified the attempt to develop a more for-ward policy. The Soviet Union's status as a global super-power has been accepted by the United States, with whom talks on the limitation of strategic arms began in 1969, and were successfully concluded (at least in a first stage) in 1972. Internally, the Soviet leadership of Brezhnev, Kosygin and Podgorny has survived for eight years, and shown every sign of stability and self-confidence, even after crises like Czecho-slovakia, the Middle East and the outbreak of border fighting on the Soviet–Chinese frontier. Soviet strategic power has been growing fast, and the Soviet Navy's peacetime politico-military activities have been expanding throughout the world. Russia's ability to broaden the military and politico-military threat against NATO has been on the increase, while the areas of traditional Soviet influence and military power remain firmly in Soviet hands.

The Soviet Union has welcomed in particular the stabilisa-tion of the strategic relationship with the United States which the Strategic Arms Limitation Treaty of May 1972 provided, not only on account of the status which it gave to the Soviet Union as a super-power, but also because of the distance it put between the two super-powers and potential claimants to this status, for example China, and possibly Western Europe, and the economic savings which it no doubt hopes will result from an end to the unrestricted strategic arms race. But the Soviet leaders also welcomed the evidence which the treaty provided of the bilateral relationship between the United States and the Soviet Union in action. Russian governments have always sought a viable working relationship with the other most powerful state in the world, and the present Soviet leadership is no exception. These leaders want it to be clearly seen that in vital matters such as security in a nuclear world, the United States and the Soviet Union, acting as equals, are ready to shoulder the responsibility of providing, stabilising and maintaining the 'nuclear umbrella' which the existence of massive numbers of nuclear weapons on both sides has created. This does not, of course, in any way rule out Soviet or Communist activities to undermine the position, or weaken the influence of the West at a lower level than the 'nuclear umbrella', or cause the Soviet Union to discontinue the unremitting ideological struggle against all who will not accept Soviet leadership or guidance in world affairs. The dual Soviet goal of a stabilisation of the strategic relationship with the United States and freedom to increase Soviet, and weaken Western and Chinese influence whenever possible is one of the fundamental factors in the development of current Soviet policies towards Europe.

Of course there are failures and difficulties on the Soviet side too; the problem of China weighs heavily on Soviet policy-making all over the world, including Europe, and the political reliability of Eastern Europe is potentially at risk – as was seen dramatically in the Polish riots of December 1970. The Soviet economy is still relatively backward (agriculture in particular being a perennial headache), and serious problems connected with resource–allocation and the need to raise the standard of living of the Soviet people are always present. But Soviet history has shown that rarely, if ever, has the internal situation, the economy, or even external threats in one sector, dissuaded confident and experienced Soviet leaders from formulating active policies elsewhere: so much of Soviet foreign policy is in practice 'compartmentalised'. As the 1970s opened, therefore, the Russians felt themselves completely justified in opting for an active foreign policy offensive in Europe; an offensive which accorded with Soviet strengths, Soviet and Russian nationalist aims and ambitions, and with the sense of political mission which still underlies the thinking of the present generation of Soviet leaders.

At the risk of over-simplifying Soviet motives and policy planning, it seems that the main aim of the Soviet Union in this European political offensive is to alter the balance of power in Europe to the advantage of the Soviet Union without endangering Soviet security by what Communist terminology calls 'adventurist' policies. The Russians want to increase the say they have in West European political and economic affairs, weakening the cohesion of the West, and trying to undermine the confidence of the populations of Western Europe in NATO. Ideally, and in the longer term, the Soviet Union would like to work towards a Europe in which the Soviet hold on Eastern Europe was unchanged, but the whole of Western Europe had adopted a different political, military and economic alignment. The Russians would like Western Europe to be made up of militarily weak nation-states, each spending very little on defence, and joined by no effective military alliance; they would like an end to the American military presence in Europe and the Mediterranean, and to existing American guarantees to West European defence. They would like economic rivalry to replace co-operation, and an end to prospects of West European political cohesion or future integration.

This is, of course, an ideal solution for the Soviet Union, and is clearly an unrealistic vision of the Europe which they would like to see. Nevertheless, it is worth bearing in mind as the long-term goal of the Soviet Union when considering the practical steps which the Russians may try to take in order to improve the balance of power in their favour. It is at this point that the Soviet Union is particularly interested in establishing a forum on European affairs through which the Russians might begin to increase their influence in Western European affairs, help to divide Western Europe and weaken the influence of NATO. The Russians apparently believe that the creation of such a forum could also help in an orderly and peaceful transition from 'Stalemate Mark I' to 'Stalemate Mark II'. The Russians would hope to have a relatively cohesive group of allies to support its attitudes and propositions in this 'forum' and would not expect to find a great deal of unanimity among its Western members, some of which would be NATO countries and other neutrals. It is very unlikely that the all-European 'institution' (to which the Russians themselves have given the title 'the All-European Commission') would in any way have executive powers, or that the Russians would in practice expect to dominate the proceedings or eliminate the freedom of action of non-Communist members. But the Soviet Union would hope to 'institutionalise' its interest in West European affairs, play a more active part in attempting to divide Western Europe, and in creating a general atmosphere of euphoria in which NATO might find it harder to retain its military strength and political cohesion. It would also hope to exclude the United States and Canada from this commission except, perhaps, as observers.

The creation of this All-European Commission is likely to remain the central theme of Soviet policy towards Western Europe during the 1970s. As an indication of its importance in Soviet eyes, the Russians have proposed a programme of activities designed to bring it about as soon as possible, and made a number of concessions to the West in the process. The Soviet Union's plan involves the calling of a European Conference on Security and Co-operation, whose preparatory phase may begin in Helsinki this autumn; the Conference itself will take place some time in 1973. According to current Soviet proposals, which have still to be discussed, the first item on the conference agenda would be a formal acceptance by all participants, including the United States and Canada, of the territorial and political settlements achieved as a result of the allied victory in the Second World War. This item could take the form of a declaration agreed by all participants, if the Soviet concept of its wording were to be adopted, it would help to keep Germany divided by securing general acceptance of East Germany as a European state, and to inhibit the West from querying the political *status quo* or the policies of the regimes in East European countries.

The second item in the Soviet proposals is concerned with the improvement of East–West trade and technological exchanges in Europe. It reflects the Soviet and East European need for Western know-how and equipment, as well as hard currency: the Russians and their allies may also be interested in seeing how far they can shorten still further the list of articles embargoed by NATO for the purposes of East–West trade, though this is not likely to be an overriding motive.

It is the third item on the Soviet agenda which is probably the most significant to the Russians. It suggests the establishment of the 'All-European Commission', through which the Soviet Union could increase its influence in Western Europe within an agreed constitutional framework, and could move gradually into the more influential conditions of 'Stalemate Mark II'. It is very important for the Russians that the 'All-European Commission' should not be imposed from outside; it should come into being by general agreement among the states of Europe, preferably with American and Canadian approval, and every effort should be made to make it look attractive, or at least harmless, to public opinion in Western Europe. Its character as a forum in which any European country can raise topics for discussion is, in fact, being emphasised in Soviet propaganda.

From the point of view of this study, the most significant factor is the energy with which the Soviet Union has pursued the goal of the holding of a European Security Conference, the skill of its diplomacy, and the concessions which it has made to the Western point of view in order to make the conference attractive. For example, the Soviet Government cleared away a number of obstacles in the way of a settlement of the Berlin problem which the Western powers could sign and, where necessary, achieve ratification by their parliaments. The Russians encouraged the East Germans to be more flexible in their talks with the West Germans, and so paved the way for an eventual East German–West German political agreement. The Soviet Union also signed a treaty with the Federal Republic, which was ratified in Bonn and Moscow this year, as was also a similar treaty between Bonn and Warsaw. Contacts have begun between Bonn and Prague, although progress here is slower, partly because of the Czechoslovak demand that the West Germans declare that the Munich agreement of 1938 was 'null and void *ab initio*' (which raises all sorts of legal problems for the Germans), and partly because of the over-cautious nature of the present Czechoslovak leadership.

All these concessions and negotiations have met most of the conditions set by NATO countries for a European Security Conference, and it seems virtually certain that it will now take place in 1973. When it does, the Soviet representatives will do all they can to see that it leads to the establishment of the 'All-European Commission'. Once the Commission is established, the Russians may want to move cautiously at first towards their long-term goal, so that West European governments and peoples will get used to the idea of the Commission's existence: for example, by initially restricting its activities to discussion of economic problems, trade and the exchange of technology. But gradually the Russians will show their hand. It is plausible to expect them fairly soon to try to use the Commission, among many other approaches, to hold up or reverse any moves towards political integration within the enlarged Common Market. The Soviet Union might also try to secure discussion in the Commission on any future applications for membership of the Common Market (for example by Spain); and at some time during the decade it is possible that the Soviet Union will raise the subject of the British position in Gibraltar, presenting it, no doubt, to the European Commission as 'the need to end the remnants of colonialism in Europe'. The Russians would hope to provoke disunity among Western countries on issues such as these. And in general, the Soviet Union would continue to appeal, within the European Commission and outside it, to the peoples of Europe over the heads of their governments, to believe in the Soviet Union's 'policy of peace', to call upon their own governments to reduce military expenditure, and to question the need for the further existence of NATO in the atmosphere of 'détente' in the wake of a Conference on European Security and Co-operation.

Although preceding paragraphs have described probable Soviet motives for a European Security Conference, the actual subject of security in the military sense has not been raised. In the early stages of its campaign for a conference, the Soviet Union stressed that a conference of this nature was not an appropriate one for the discussion of military and security affairs, which would best be left to a specialist group, perhaps set up by the 'All-European Commission'. In practical terms, European security turns on the subject of mutual and balanced force reductions (M.B.F.R.), on which NATO offered proposals in 1968 – which remained unanswered for three years. In May 1971 the Soviet Party leader Brezhnev also offered talks on M.B.F.R. 'in a suitable forum'; but it also became clear that what the Soviet Union really wanted was a bilateral discussion of the subject with the United States, rather like the Strategic Arms Limitation Talks, with each side informing its allies as appropriate. The Americans of course would not consider talks on this basis, but there seems to be some consensus that the best forum for talks on M.B.F.R. would be some kind of specialist committee, rather than the full-scale Security Conference.

Since any negotiations on M.B.F.R. which do take place will probably last well into the mid-1970s, it may be worth outlining the Soviet attitude to force reductions in Europe, that is, to European security in its present form. The Soviet Union has had, and will continue to have, three main reasons for maintaining its forces in Europe: first, to ensure that the countries of Eastern Europe remain in the hands of loyal pro-Soviet Communist regimes; second, to provide for the defence of the Soviet Union's western border as far to the west as possible; and third, should deterrence fail, to allow the Soviet forces to take the initiative against NATO in any European campaign. In deciding the number of troops which they would need in Eastern Europe at any one time, the Russians clearly cannot fall below a certain minimum to ensure their political control in Eastern Europe, but might adapt their total above this figure in accordance with the number of American units in Western Europe. One of the basic aims of the Soviet Union, in my view, is to see the end of NATO and the total withdrawal of American forces from Europe – and indeed, the end of the American guarantee to Western Europe's defence. The Soviet Union will therefore favour the kind of negotiations on M.B.F.R. which will encourage the United States to withdraw the maximum number of troops from Europe. These troops, in Soviet calculations, include the Sixth Fleet in the Mediterranean.

It seems reasonable therefore to expect to see the Soviet Union probing the possibilities of M.B.F.R. with the Americans, whose contribution to NATO in Europe they regard as the linchpin of West European defence. They do not really believe that it is worth negotiating seriously with the other members of NATO unless the theme of American reductions is central, and Soviet preference is still for direct negotiations with the United States. We cannot predict how M.B.F.R. talks might take place or evolve; if the Russians cannot persuade the Americans to talk bilaterally, their second preference would be for multi-lateral talks within the framework of the 'All-European Commission' or a specialist committee meeting independently of the European Security Conference. What the Russians want to avoid if possible is a conference on M.B.F.R. in which NATO discusses the problem with the Warsaw Pact, alliance to alliance. This method of negotiating would prevent the Soviet negotiators from attempting to divide the individual members of NATO and so gaining tactical advantages; but it would also 'violate' the principle of bilateralism by introducing more broadly-based organisations, NATO and the Warsaw Pact, into discussions on security: and this the Soviet Union would oppose.

In the final analysis, the Soviet leaders probably contrast their ability to retain military forces beyond their frontiers in Europe with the economic and political difficulties which are likely to face American administrations on this subject, which the Russians probably believe may become increasingly severe, and lead to unilateral American force withdrawals in the fairly near future. The Soviet Union has few problems, either politically or economically, in keeping its forces in Europe at whatever level its leaders believe is necessary: the Soviet ground forces are over 160 divisions strong, and 20 or 30 divisions of these deployed in Eastern Europe is no strain to a country with forces of that size, the reserves of trained manpower available and the vast stocks of weapons and equipment in the Soviet inventory. There is, moreover, another point here: although the Soviet Union could bring its forces back into Eastern Europe from Soviet territory in an emergency much more easily than the Americans could send theirs across the Atlantic to Western Europe from the United States, it is very unlikely that the Soviet Union would withdraw all its troops from Eastern Europe; this is especially true of East Germany, which must always be maintained as a separate state and where the Russians would probably always want to have a controlling garrison, in view of the sensitivity of the German problem, regardless of the number of American troops in the West. An Eastern Europe without any Soviet troops is therefore a very remote possibility.

So far this paper has outlined what I believe to be the main direction of Soviet policy-making towards Europe, and has attempted to describe positive Soviet political aims and the means by which the Russians hope to achieve them. While it is true that in broad terms the Soviet Union is on the offensive politically in Europe, this does not mean that some of their policy is not reactive to events in the West. For example, the Russians appear to believe that they are more likely to win a more favourable response to their policy in German official circles from a Social Democratic Federal German Government than from a possible alternative regime; and therefore they have had to hurry along some of their German policies, offering, earlier in 1972, greater inducements from ratification of the Bonn–Moscow treaty than East Germany would have liked.

Similarly, the Soviet Union will have to react to the enlargement of the Common Market. The Russians have always opposed the Common Market, and especially its enlargement, as an operation designed to strengthen the capitalist economies of Western Europe. They are also afraid of its possible development into a political or even military organisation. But they certainly realise that there is little that they can do to halt its expansion as an economic entity, and they will have to adapt some of their policies in Europe to take the enlarged Common Market into account.

In this context, the Soviet Union will be primarily interested in preventing or slowing down any moves to turn the Market into a politically integrated unit, and in ensuring that its commercial policy does not damage Soviet prospects for increased bilateral trade with individual members of the Common Market. In the first case, the Russians will try to encourage those members of the Market who are less enthusiastic about political integration, perhaps in some cases by offering political or economic concessions. In the second instance, in which the Soviet Union places considerable emphasis on East–West trade, especially in the field of advanced equipment and management techniques, the

Russians will try to support countries who are anxious to classify trade with state-trading nations (that is, the Communist powers) as 'political activity', and therefore outside the regulations embodied in the Treaty of Rome on this issue. However, in all its reactions to developments connected with the Common Market, the Soviet Union probably realises that it can fight only rearguard actions, and that Soviet opposition can hardly be decisive; but it would not be in the nature of the Soviet Union as we know it to give up or to fail to probe the Common Market in search of weak points or divisive factors in its make-up.

So much for the overall political aims of the Soviet Union. In pursuing these aims the Soviet Union relies to a considerable extent upon its military strength and the pressures which it can bring to bear against NATO, and therefore the Russians will strive to maintain and improve their military posture in the European 'theatre' throughout the 1970s.

Since the Soviet armed forces and their Warsaw Pact allies enjoy military superiority in Central Europe, with their 31 divisions and considerable air forces (each country bordering on a NATO power in Central Europe has a Soviet garrison) backed up by Soviet naval and strategic missile forces in the Soviet Union, the Soviet aim will probably be to retain this superiority by a programme of weapon and equipment replacement on a continuing basis. We have already mentioned the point that the actual numbers of divisions or troops stationed in Eastern Europe could vary according to the number of American troops in Western Europe, and that there will always be a requirement for a minimum Soviet force in the East in order to ensure the political loyalty of the East European countries. Whatever the strength of the Soviet forces in Central Europe, their effectiveness will be maintained at the highest possible level through training, exercises and re-equipment. This will probably be a cornerstone of Soviet military policy in Europe throughout the 1970s.

In broad terms, the Soviet strategy for the improvement of its military posture vis-à-vis NATO is, while maintaining military superiority in Central Europe, to try to squeeze NATO's flanks, exerting greater pressure in peacetime from the north, and the south and south-east. The pressure of

NATO's northern flank will be mainly a high-seas threat: the Soviet Union will try to push its 'maritime frontier' further and further into the Atlantic, trying, as it were, to 'mark off' greater areas of the North Atlantic and the Arctic Ocean as areas primarily of Soviet naval activity, and to make them as difficult of access, by intense surveillance for example, for NATO fleets as possible. The whole concept of 'enclosing' or 'delimitating' areas of the high seas, while not effective in keeping other navies out (for example, the NATO policy of sending naval vessels into the Black Sea from time to time), is characteristic of Soviet politico-military thought, and the Russians are likely to continue to pursue it.

It also has some relevance to the south and south-east flanks, where Soviet propaganda is beginning to claim that the Soviet Navy has more 'right' in the Eastern Mediterranean than NATO navies. It is on this flank that the Soviet pressure has been most dramatic in recent years, and may well develop further during the decade. Here the Soviet Union maintains a combat squadron of from 35 to 75 ships in the Mediterranean on permanent station, including submarines, missile-firing cruisers, landing craft and, normally, a helicopter ship. Until recently the squadron had reconnaissance (and potentially strike) air support from bases in Egypt, and at least two ports in Egypt where its ships could call for replenishment and recreation, and there is evidence that part of the Soviet facilities in Egypt related specially to air support for anti-submarine warfare.

It is impossible to predict at this stage what effect the withdrawal of Soviet military personnel from Egypt in July 1972 will have on this support for the Soviet Mediterranean Squadron. But it seems certain that the Russians will at some time in the future resume the search for facilities which they will be able to use for surveillance and possibly strike purposes against Western fleets in the Mediterranean and the Indian Ocean.

The enforced withdrawal of Soviet military personnel from Egypt showed that the Soviet Union's military posture against NATO in the Mediterranean area may suffer a setback at any time through the uncertainties and instabilities of the countries of the area, and it is always possible that an upset in

Soviet–Arab relations could damage or weaken Soviet facilities or access rights in the area. But it seems likely that the
Soviet leaders will press ahead with the strengthening of their
sea–air capabilities along the whole of NATO's southern
flank. They will try, by political and economic means, to
protect themselves against the loss of facilities in Mediterranean countries, and they will watch events in Libya,
Tunisia, Algeria and Malta with particular care for signs of
political change (e.g. a revolution in Tunisia or further differences between Malta and Britain) which they might exploit.
Later on in the decade the Russians may try to extend their
influence more directly into the Western Mediterranean,
with attempts to raise our position in Gibraltar, both within
and outside the 'All-European Commission', playing an
important role.

The future of Yugoslavia and Albania will also be of
importance to the Soviet Union during the 1970s. While the
Russians have probably learnt the lesson that direct military
threats to intervene in Yugoslavia after the departure of
President Tito would be the surest way to unite all Yugoslavs
against the Soviet Union, Soviet political intrigues cannot be
ruled out; if successful, they, and skilfully selective promises
of economic aid, could, in certain circumstances, affect the
cohesion of the Yugoslav state. The Soviet Union rarely for-
gets an injury, and no Soviet leader is likely to have abandoned for ever the idea of the return of Yugoslavia and
Albania to the pro-Soviet fold.

I believe that the main theme of Soviet policy towards
Western Europe during the 1970s is likely to be the successful transition from the 1949 'Stalemate Mark I' to 'Stalemate
Mark II', a stable position of authority in Europe appropriate
to the only European super-power. In essence, this is a
political operation, to be carried out patiently and skilfully
by diplomacy and negotiation; it aims, by means of a European Security Conference, to obtain general European
agreement to the establishment of a permanent 'All-European
Commission' through which the Soviet Union could exercise greater influence over West European affairs, and help
to create an atmosphere of 'détente' in which NATO would
(in Soviet eyes) have to fight hard for its existence. In the

much longer term, the Russians would like to see a Europe in which the East is firmly under their control, and the West divided and militarily weak, without American troops or an American defence guarantee.

At the same time, this political offensive must be accompanied by a retention of existing military capabilities, and their improvement if possible, and further pressure against NATO, especially against its northern and southern flanks. While the Russians are ready to reduce the number of their forces in Eastern Europe in accordance with the strength of the American forces in the West, and are prepared to discuss reductions at international conferences, reductions are not essential to them for political, military or economic reasons, and any talks may be prolonged and geared more to American attitudes in Washington than to European factors. Throughout the decade the Soviet Union will aim to maintain and if possible to improve its military posture vis-à-vis NATO in Europe.

There are, however, some inherent weaknesses in the Soviet position which, because of the nature of some of them, have fallen outside the scope of this study. For example, although I have made some conservative assumptions about the Soviet leadership, it is always possible that internal factors in the Soviet system may affect the authority of the leadership and express themselves in a slackening of Soviet foreign policy initiatives. It is also possible that preoccupation with China may influence Soviet European policies, but this is not likely to be a major factor in the short to medium term. Some of the strength of the present Soviet position in the Mediterranean area depends on factors largely outside Soviet control, and Soviet policies may be affected by changes of allegiance in the Arab world.

In a more direct sense, the Soviet political offensive may not make the progress expected of it because of political and economic factors in Western Europe. The Soviet Union cannot seriously influence the development of the Common Market, or the results of parliamentary elections in West European countries, of which the most important may be those in West Germany. But perhaps most interesting of all, if the Western powers approach the European Security

Conference, the talks on force reductions and the establishment of an 'All-European Commission' in a positive frame of
mind, using all their deep experience of negotiating with the
Soviet Union both in the preparatory work and in the meetings themselves, there is no reason why the Soviet case should
win by default. If the West remains united, the Soviet political offensive should be regarded as an acceptable challenge,
which we can meet with good chances of success in uphold-
ing our essential standards and values in the Western Europe
of the future.

4

European Security and an Enlarged Community

JOHN C. GARNETT*

This paper seeks to explore some of the defence implications of an enlarged Community by examining the international environment in which it must operate, by speculating about the sort of international behaviour it will adopt, and by analysing the collaborative ventures which its members may undertake. At the outset it is worth emphasing that there is a sense in which an enlarged European Community has no defence implications whatever. Formally, membership of the E.E.C. carries no obligations other than a customs union, an agreed agricultural policy and a common commercial policy, and one has only to consider the policies of the present members to see that in itself membership carries no strategic or military implications. Furthermore, there is some evidence that the Common Market countries, particularly France, are much more interested in the fields of commerce and finance than they are in security. The enlargement of the Community may herald significant economic changes but very few developments in the defence field. When we talk about the defence implications of the Common Market, we are not, therefore, talking about inevitable consequences. We are simply speculating about possibilities, about what might happen if member states extended to the political and military fields the sort of arrangements which have proved so mutually beneficial in the economic field. Inevitably, what follows is a mixture of what is and what may be, of ideas tempered with realism, of long-term goals shelved for

* Senior Lecturer in International Politics, University College of Wales, Aberystwyth, and academic consultant to the National Defence College.

short-term achievements. And throughout it all there is a clear recognition that politics is the art of the possible in pursuit of the desirable.

Since the Second World War, and in retrospect at least, Europe has been one of the most stable areas of the world. Frontiers have been frozen, and the clash of super-powers across what used to be called the Iron Curtain has helped to rigidify political as well as military postures. And although countries on both sides of a divided Europe have made impressive economic progress, politically and militarily European power and influence have been in steady decline. Moscow, Washington and Peking have now eclipsed London, Berlin and Paris as the major centres of international decision-making, and Europe, divided and dominated by two super-powers facing each other in Berlin and Germany, has been a relatively quiet and increasingly introspective continent.

Recently, however, as confrontation has given way to détente, and as the forces of polycentrism have undermined the unity of the two blocs which have dominated European politics, it appears that Europe is once more on the move. The language and terminology of the Cold War have passed into history, and the talk today is of force reductions and security conferences. As bipolarity gives way to a more flexible system, European states may discover a new freedom to mould their futures and to devise new political, economic and military arrangements more appropriate to the last quarter of the twentieth century.

It may be useful to outline some of the fundamental changes which are creating this environment of flux in which genuine options may become available to European states for the first time for many years. At the same time it may be worth noting that periods of change, although they undoubtedly create opportunities, also contain dangers. Those who are sensitive to these dangers, and dubious about the capacity of European statesmen to exploit the opportunities, tend to regret the passing of a polarised Europe dominated by hostile super-powers. Quite rightly they point out that whatever injustices and inhumanities were enshrined in the Cold War, the military and political confrontation of the two great alliance systems at least provided the basis for an enduring peace in a traditionally unstable area. The two alliances have managed to contain or suppress innumerable potentially dangerous conflicts which have simmered beneath the surface of European politics both within and between the two blocs. Through the alliances which they controlled or dominated the two super-powers have been able to influence and discipline their European allies, but it seems reasonable to assume that as their grip slackens, intra-European conflicts and tensions will once more bubble to the surface.

Under the strain of détente and a much more ambiguous threat, both NATO and the Warsaw Pact are under considerable pressure. In Eastern Europe the forces of independence and polycentrism are a permanent threat to the authority of the Soviet Union, and in the West the diminishing psychological and physical commitment of the United States to Western Europe will have profound effects on the North Atlantic alliance. What is happening is that though the formal bipolar alliance structure of European politics remains intact, it no longer corresponds very closely to the political realities of a more fluid Europe. In general terms, Pierre Hassner has explained the situation very clearly: 'Existing authorities and structures keep their formal status and the physical means of power but are unable to satisfy either the political and psychological demands for participation and self-expression, or the technological and economic demands for efficiency, which emanate from their followers or subjects.'[1] Beneath the familiar surface of European politics, both within and between countries, considerable new and probably unmanageable socio-political forces are at work. The turbulence and bitterness of modern industrial relations, the resurgence of minority conflicts and widespread student unrest are all symptoms of the forces of change which are detectable throughout Europe. Already they have created a general crisis of authority and legitimacy, and few can doubt that they will push Europe into a very different environment in the 1980s.

The existence of potentially destructive forces not too far beneath the surface of European politics should not be

[1] P. Hassner, 'The New Europe: From Cold War to Hot Peace', *International Journal*, xxvii, 1 (Winter 1971–2) 8.

allowed to obscure more positive and creative achievements.
In particular, the development of the European Economic
Community must rank as one of the most imaginative and
hopeful ventures in post-war politics. Its impetus came from
far-sighted and perceptive Europeans who recognised that
nation-states of the size and scale of those in Western Europe
were no longer able to deal adequately with the problems
which confronted them. John Herz has pointed out that there
are now a large range of functions, including the safeguard-
ing of the security of its citizens and promoting their economic welfare, that the independent sovereign state is
incapable of performing on its own. In the nuclear age all
states are more or less vulnerable to attack, and in a
complicated trading world economic prosperity depends
upon trade cycles, exchange rates, terms of trade and economic growth in other states rather than upon government
policy.

Putting it crudely, the sovereign state – particularly the
non-super-power sovereign state – already partly discredited
by the excesses of nationalism, is, in the modern world of
mass markets, super-powers, missiles, expensive technology
and large-scale industrial techniques, a functional anachron-
ism. Those who acknowledged this basic fact sought new
forms of organisation which were not based on the exclusive
rights of each state but upon the need for joint action and
closer unity. The European Community is a very real mani-
festation of their aspirations, and already it has made deep
inroads into the traditional structure of some of the most
important states in Western Europe. This is not intended to
imply that the nation-state has lost its appeal as an emotional
symbol and mystical focus for the loyalty and affection of
millions of Europeans; but it does mean that an important,
new and rapidly developing actor has appeared on the European and world stage. As the Community is enlarged from
six to nine members it seems likely that further impetus will
be given to the integration movement, and inevitably, as the
Community becomes more involved in political questions,
problems of defence and foreign policy are bound to arise.
The international role that this new actor will seek to play is
uncertain, but like that of all states, it is bound to be circum-

scribed by the attitudes and policies of those states with which it has to deal.

Antony Hartley is probably right in his suggestion that 'a political Europe beginning to emerge in the late seventies will be liable to discover its freedom of action limited by international decisions in which it has had no say and which its component parts have been too weak to affect'.[2] In particular, the freedom of Europe to shape its own destiny may be seriously undermined both by the policies of the super-powers and by the rise of non-European states to positions of power and influence in world affairs. However unpalatable it might have been to such old-fashioned nationalists as de Gaulle, Europe is no longer the cockpit of the world, and her future will be determined by decisions taken outside Europe as well as those in Europe. So far as Europe's future is concerned, Senator Mansfield is at least as important as Chancellor Brandt and President Pompidou, and few would doubt that Mr Nixon and Mr Kosygin are more important than both of them.

The respective policies of the two super-powers towards Europe form very obvious constraints on the freedom of European states, either individually or collectively, to pursue their interests. What is not so obvious is that the European policies of both the Soviet Union and the United States are very much influenced by their relationship with each other. It is for this reason that détente – always likely to develop into an exclusive, bilateral super-power relationship – has always been a mixed blessing for Europe. So long as the United States and the Soviet Union continue to allocate the highest priority to improving their relationship with each other, European interests are bound to look vulnerable and European politicians are bound to feel uneasy. Indeed, suspicion, however vague and unjustified, of super-power collusion if not condominium will provide a very real motive for European unity if it transpires that the Soviets and the Americans are prepared to ride roughshod over European interests. As the super-powers become reluctant to jeopardise the détente which has sprung up between them for the sake

[2] A. Hartley, 'Europe between the Super-Powers', *Foreign Affairs*, XLIX, 2 (Jan 1971) 272.

of purely European interests, the European states may find
that only those policies which do not involve the super-
powers in any risks can command acceptance, let alone positive support.

It may sound a little fanciful – though de Gaulle did not
think it so – to speculate on the nightmare possibility of
positive American–Soviet co-operation or collusion at the
expense of Europe. But it is certainly true that the combined
pressure and influence of the two super-powers could make
savage inroads into Europe's freedom to manoeuvre. Even
without any malevolent co-operation, the super-powers wield
enormous, perhaps decisive, power in European affairs. And
it is surely fair to suggest that a developing Europe must not
count either on the continuing passivity of the Soviet Union
or the continuing benevolence of the United States towards
European integration.

The Soviet Union has never looked with equanimity upon
the emergence of a resurgent Europe. The prospect of a
powerful and possibly hostile super-power on their western
as well as eastern frontiers is a daunting proposition for Soviet
leaders, and it is not surprising, therefore, that Soviet hostility
towards all attempts at European integration, including the
Common Market, has been a consistent feature of their diplomacy. Although they may have relinquished any ideas of
territorial conquest in Western Europe, the Soviets recognise
that only by keeping Europe divided and weak can they hope
to exercise preponderant influence. There is no need to suppose that the Soviets will take physical steps to prevent the
emergence of a powerful Western Europe, even one with a
European Defence Community of some sort, but it seems fair
to assume that whatever progress is made in this direction
will be without their help and, indeed, in spite of considerable diplomatic opposition.

Needless to say, Soviet hostility to the idea of a Europe
which is integrated militarily as well as economically should
not be used as an argument for not pressing ahead with it.
European states are not yet so overshadowed by their super-
power neighbour that policies have to be tailored to please
her. No doubt the Soviets will wax eloquent on the subject of
German militarism and American imperialism, but in effect

moves towards European defence integration are unlikely to cause more than a ripple on the smooth waters of détente. After all, as François Duchêne has pointed out, there is nothing provocative about improving one's minimum security arrangements.[3]

The attitude of the United States is a good deal more equivocal. Traditionally, the United States has enthusiastically supported the idea of European integration and independence. Successive Presidents have extolled the virtues of a new and independent centre of power able and willing to act in harmony with the United States and to shoulder world-wide responsibilities. President Kennedy's 'twin pillar' idea at Atlantic partnership reflected this persistent strand in American foreign policy, and as recently as 1971 President Nixon reaffirmed his support for the idea: 'The United States has always supported the strengthening and enlargement of the European Community. We still do. We welcome cohesion in Europe because it makes Europe a sturdier pillar of the structure of peace.'[4]

It may be too cynical to suggest that some American proponents of European unity see a successful political and military entity on this side of the Atlantic as a good excuse for sliding out of their NATO commitments. But it is certainly true that an improved level of competence and effort in the European part of NATO would make it easier for the United States to press ahead with its planned withdrawals. Once again, this should not be used as ammunition against European defence integration. Whether the Europeans sort themselves out or not, the United States is likely to reduce its commitment. Prolonging Europe's weakness is unlikely to delay the process, and conceivably, by irritating the Americans, may actually hasten it.

But the real implications of a united Europe have only recently been thought through in the United States. Very few supporters of European unity seemed to realise that even a *potential* super-power would be more difficult to manage than a divided conglomeration of independent sovereign

[3] F. Duchêne, 'A New European Defence Community', *Foreign Affairs*, L, 1 (Oct 1971) 81.
[4] Richard Nixon, 'U.S. Foreign Policy for the 1970s' (Feb 1971) p. 29.

states, and even fewer contemplated the very real possibility that the interests of a united Europe might well diverge sharply from those of the United States. Some of these possibilities are now keenly appreciated in Washington, and although officially the government is still well disposed towards the idea of a united Europe, the idea of 'partnership' has a hollow ring to it and there are plenty of signs of diminishing enthusiasm.

Many Americans are openly worried about the policies which an inward-looking, introspective Europe might follow, and they have been particularly agitated by the trade-discrimination policies of the E.E.C. Obviously, the development of a unitary, preferential trading bloc comprising most of Western Europe and linked by preferential trade agreements to Africa and the Mediterranean could have serious consequences for the United States economy. The American Government has already reacted quite sharply, and it is clear that the future will see some very hard bargaining over a whole range of trade problems. It is reasonable to suppose that as the economic costs of supporting Europe impinge more heavily on the United States economy, the government may find it increasingly difficult to justify its political support for European unity. A slightly worsening trade relationship might be regarded as a fair price to pay for the achievement of more important political goals, but when even these are being questioned, criticism is inevitable. It is difficult to avoid R. Cooper's[5] conclusion that although the United States has supported the unification of Europe, including Britain, for the past quarter century, dispassionate analysis may question the wisdom of this position for the last half of that period.

It is arguable that the international implications inherent in a united Europe are even more profound than is generally appreciated either in the Soviet Union or the United States. A great deal will depend upon the *kind* of Europe which develops. Joining the European Community is a bit like stepping on an escalator travelling at variable speed towards an unknown but, hopefully, desirable destination. So far political scientists have not reflected very much on the nature of a

[5] R. Cooper, 'The U.S. and the Enlarged European Community', *The Round Table*, no. 244 (Oct 1971) p. 576.

united Europe. They have accepted unity as a self-evidently virtuous goal and they have been too obsessed by the problems of bringing it about to think very much about how it might behave.

It may be that the Europe which emerges will be a 'low profile' Europe, fairly introspective and content to jog along between the super-powers and in uneasy partnership with one of them. But a much more assertive Europe is a long-term possibility which cannot be ignored. Indeed, the political will and energy which are required to unite Europe in the first place are precisely the qualities likely to push her into an active and positive world role. Western Europe is already one of the wealthiest pieces of real estate in the world. The Community of Nine will have a combined G.N.P. of over £250,000 million, and a very high level of industrial development. Militarily speaking it can muster more than 2 million men under arms, some strategic nuclear capability, powerful air forces and, apart from the super-powers, the strongest naval forces in the world. Potentially, Western Europe is in the super-power league, and if unity should fire her ambition, her influence and importance could be enormous. The development of a 'third force' Europe, anxious to engage in the traditional power-political game and equipped with nuclear weapons and super-power confidence and ambition, could not fail to have the most profound effects on global strategy and the pattern of world politics. It is idle to suppose that the emergence of such a super-state would be regarded with either equanimity or approval in many parts of the world.

Super-power Europe, a vast regional bloc, playing, on a grand scale, the age-old game of nation-states, is not what the original architects of the European Community had in mind. And there are many Europeans who feel uneasy about such a role. They would prefer a more obviously *virtuous* Europe, probably a non-nuclear Europe, outward-looking in the sense of showing proper concern for the development of the Third World, but not outward-looking in the sense of being willing to acquire and use military power in the pursuit of its interests around the world. Whether, in a society of independent sovereign states, a militarily castrated Europe makes political sense is doubtful. Traditionally most states, even neutrals, have found the possession of military power an indispensable instrument of survival in a world which, if not hostile, is frequently apathetic towards the fate of those who cannot fend for themselves.

But 'great-power Europe', militarily on the same footing as the super-powers, is, if it is possible at all, in the distant future. In terms of practical politics, the plain fact of the matter is that Europe is now, and is likely to remain in the foreseeable future, dependent upon the United States for strategic and conventional military power. Although, as a result of the present reappraisal, the American–European relationship is likely to undergo some readjustment, Europe's dependence is likely to continue to be one of the most important constraints on her freedom to manoeuvre. While it exists it is impossible to think of Europe pursuing policies with which the United States seriously disagrees. There is therefore no question of Europe acting independently of her major ally, and no question of dismantling the major alliance which links them.

NATO is the cornerstone of Western defence, and though one may look forward to the development within NATO of a consciously European caucus, the alliance will continue to provide the major institutional framework for the operational aspects of European defence. The Community's growing interest in foreign and defence policy need not undermine the alliance's fundamental role in Europe, though it may lead to developments within the alliance which will help put the European–American relationship on a steadier and more balanced footing.

The precise nature of united Europe is not yet clear, but there is mounting evidence that it will not be one in which there are strong and powerful supra-national institutions. The supra-national, Monnetist philosophy which was so popular in the early years has taken some hard knocks from contemporary politicians – particularly in Britain and France where there is widespread fear of a Europe characterised by institutional dogmatism and illiberal bureaucracy. Mr Heath reassured a good many people when, in reporting his conversations with M. Pompidou in May 1971, he spoke of their agreement that 'the identity of national states should be

maintained in the framework of the developing community ...
the processes of harmonisation should not override essential
national interests'.

Mr Heath's 'minimalist' pragmatic vision of European
unity has been elaborated in his 1967 Godkin Lectures at
Harvard, but in some ways it is an ambiguous and unsatisfactory conception. On the one hand he is clearly unwilling
to contemplate a straight federal solution, a unitary European
state with super-power potential, but on the other hand he
appears to recognise that the Community is not just another
co-operative association of independent sovereign states.[6] Mr
Heath has spoken enthusiastically about the idea of Community involvement in the fields of foreign policy and
defence, and he has quoted with approval Robert Menzies'
comment that 'a customs union cannot stand still and has no
alternative but to go forward to democratic control or back to
national systems'.[7] The Prime Minister obviously recognises
that the E.E.C. is a political reality of a quite different order
to, say, NATO. As Leonard Beaton has noted,[8] Mr Heath
seems to be advocating an entirely new political animal, an
institutional arrangement which goes far deeper than NATO
or any existing co-operative association, but which stops short
of being a state. Whether such an institution makes either
practical or even theoretical sense as a permanent goal is
rather doubtful, though as a transitional phase it can clearly
be defended.

In fact the Common Market has already acquired certain,
albeit weak, supra-national features. In the Council of
Ministers, for example, there is already a system of qualified
majority voting. And the Commission, which represents the
Community as a whole, is, because of its independent role as
initiator of Community policy, defender of Community
interests and executor of Community decisions, a qualitatively
different kind of body from traditional international secre-
tariats. The European states have already created political
institutions which limit their sovereign independence.

[6] Edward Heath, *Old World, New Horizons* (London: Oxford Univ. Press,
1970).   [7] Ibid., p. 55.
[8] Leonard Beaton, 'The Strategic Issues', in Douglas Evans (ed.), *Destiny
or Delusion* (London: Gollancz, 1971) p. 176.

However, although the sovereignty issue is at the heart of European Community politics, it is easy to make too much of it. The truth of the matter is that in the modern world medium-sized powers, even though they retain the formal apparatus of sovereignty, have already lost a good deal of their scope for practical political choice. Forces external to the state are circumscribing the freedom of all but the most powerful, and sovereignty in the practical sense of freedom to determine one's destiny, as opposed to the legal sense, is already deeply eroded. Joining the Common Market simply means having rather less of something which no one has very much of anyway.

It is almost certainly an illusion to believe that in a developing European Community critical decision-making power can remain a monopoly of national governments. Even a purely economic community is really a political phenomenon. Walter Hallstein was almost right when he said: 'We are not in business, we are in politics.'[9] In reality the two cannot be separated. Though some politicians may delude themselves, the gradual reshaping of economic relations between member countries is a process which inexorably whittles away their sovereign independence until, almost without anyone realising it, a point is reached when independent action becomes a physical impossibility, and sovereignty a complete fiction. David Mitrany was one of the first to see the significance of this. His so-called 'functional approach' to integration avoided the politically sensitive issue of sovereignty by concentrating on limited, practical arrangements which undermine sovereign independence without ever raising the issue.[10] Mr Heath's essentially Gaullist idea of a 'Europe of states' does not avoid the problem of sovereignty; it merely avoids making a political issue of it until it is too late to do anything about it. What will happen in the case of the European Community is that although individual members will retain actual and legal control over their instruments of policy, they will discover that these

[9] W. Hallstein, quoted by R. Pryce in *The Political Future of the European Community* (London: John Marshbank, 1962) p. 20.

[10] D. Mitrany, 'The Functional Approach to World Organisation', *International Affairs* (July 1948) pp. 351–60.

instruments lose their effectiveness. States will find themselves able to pursue their objectives, but quite unable to
achieve them. To take an extreme case, as the Europeans
become more mixed up in each others' economic, military and
political affairs, as national economies become more un-
balanced and as joint defence projects proliferate, it is possible to imagine a situation in which individual European
states which have retained their freedom to declare war, find,
when the crunch comes, that they are unable to wage it
simply because of the degree to which they have become
inextricably involved with partners who are now unwilling
to support them.

The gist of the argument so far has been to suggest that
while there may be no immediate strategic consequences to
an enlarged European Community, as the members become
increasingly involved in each others' material interests and
affairs they will create a community of needs and interests
which have very real defence and foreign policy implications.
As David Owen recently put it, 'On any rational basis it is
inconceivable that, in the long term, defence will be excluded
from the movement towards European integration. . .'[11]

After all, it is quite inconsistent to aim, on the one hand, at
a Common Market with the fullest possible division of labour
on a continental scale, and on the other hand to pour money
and research into purely national defence programmes. The
national and independent control of defence is frequently
regarded as the ultimate symbol of sovereignty, but the sheer
waste in terms of duplicated effort and misallocated resources
makes this one of the most expensive myths of our time. The
separation of defence from other aspects of economic planning has already led to a very artificial – and expensive –
dichotomy between civil and military research. On the civil
side the Common Market is already involved in planning and
funding a long list of high-technology projects, some of which
will involve work which overlaps essential research in the
defence field. Somehow, in the interests of economy, ways
must be found for merging under the same authority all high-
technology research for both civil and military projects.

A fully fledged European Defence Community (E.D.C.)

[11] D. Owen, *The Politics of Defence* (London: Cape, 1972) p. 195.

to complement the Common Market is a logical, if somewhat ambitious, goal, and its virtues are considerable. It could ensure the most effective collective use of national resources to provide a well-equipped and balanced European Army, backed, if necessary, by strategic nuclear capability of some significance. It could encourage member states to 'unbalance' their national forces in the interests of efficiency and specialisation. It could produce a unified European strategic posture, and by ironing out differences in tactical doctrine it could enable European forces to be deployed across national frontiers to the best possible defensive positions. It could organise the rationalisation of defence procurement on an international basis, enforce standardisation in weaponry and equipment, improve logistics, and in every respect enable the European to get value for money in the defence field. By rationally exploiting the very considerable defence effort of nine European states, a powerful E.D.C. could make Europe a genuine centre of power and a counterbalance to American power in NATO. Inevitably, an E.D.C. voice would carry a good deal of weight not just in NATO, but in the world at large.

However, it would be quite wrong to believe that the enlargement of the European Community will lead automatically to the creation of such a defence community. As a long-term objective an E.D.C. makes good sense, but in the immediate future, while Europe is politically and psychologically fragmented and without any clear sense of purpose in its external relations, it is difficult to see how a community could operate effectively. With the Hague summit of 1969 and the efforts of the Davignon Committee, the Common Market countries have begun the process of harmonising and co-ordinating their foreign policies vis-à-vis the outside world, but they are years away from agreeing upon the sort of unified European foreign policy which alone can provide a satisfactory justification and rationale for a European defence policy. Hedley Bull has reminded us that 'in international politics outside Europe the countries of Western Europe have no common policy',[12] and he might have added that even

[12] Hedley Bull, 'Europe and the Wider World', *The Round Table*, 244 (Oct 1971) p. 455.

within Europe there are sufficient discrepancies in national policies to make military co-operation very difficult. So long as the French continue to pursue an essentially Gaullist policy, it is difficult to see how either foreign or defence policies could be satisfactorily integrated. Certainly it is impossible to reconcile an E.D.C. with Debré's denial of any European identity, and his comment that 'life throughout the world is based, and will be based in coming years, upon nation-states, and the foundation of all security for men, women and their homes will be the political and military ability of the nation-states to guarantee, in so far as that is possible, their security'.[13] This philosophy precludes any kind of integration and Debré has been quite frank about his objections. He points out that in any common organisation

> there will be the integrated who follow, and the integrator who commands. . . . There may be different degrees of integration, but the principle of the distinction between the government responsible for the grouping and the others, servants or colleagues, is the same, as are all its consequences . . . which create a hierarchy of interests to the profit of the strongest who is, in the final analysis, the sole master of the security or insecurity of the group.[14]

Though not so well articulated in other countries, this kind of reasoning has a fairly wide appeal and the sentiments and feeling on which it is based constitute a formidable, if not insurmountable, obstacle to any immediate defence community. Lord Balniel is surely right in his view that establishing some sort of identity of political aims and policies must predate an integrated defence organisation: 'Fully effective defence collaboration must depend on the merging and harmonisation of wider political aims.'[15] It may be that only when there is a common feeling of nationality, when people in England feel as deeply about affairs in Paris as they do about events in London, is there a sufficiently stable political

[13] Michel Debré, 'The Principles of Our Defence Policy', reprinted in *Survival*, XII, 11 (Nov 1970) 378.
[14] Ibid., p. 379.
[15] Lord Balniel, 'European Defence and European Security', *Survival*, XIII, 5 (May 1971) 169.

basis on which to build a defence community. Some federal-
ists would dispute this by arguing that the creation of the
appropriate organisation will help bring about the political
conditions necessary for its successful operation. But when
one considers the cross-currents of European politics and the
deep divisions of ideology and philosophy within a community which will encompass the traditions of both Catholic
and Protestant Europe and such diverse ideas as liberal
democracy and organised Communism, the problems are
formidable.[16]

The difficulties are exacerbated by the fact that in the
defence field it is impossible to start from scratch. Those who
planned and created the European Economic Community did
not have to compete with an existing customs union; they
started with a clean slate. But in the defence field a new
organisation would enjoy no comparable advantage. It would
have to develop alongside existing defence arrangements
which are well established and which cannot be easily dis-
mantled or incorporated in a new set-up. The European web
of complex, if untidy, defence arrangements is dominated by
NATO and its militarily active members. Within it, but not
of it, is the recently created Euro-group which facilitates
multilateral defence co-operation at a very practical level
between its ten members. A slightly different net is provided
by the W.E.U., which has seven members including France
and a residual number of defence and arms-control functions.
In addition to these formal structures there is an elaborate
network of bilateral co-operation at the military and politico-
military levels. In Europe there is already a considerable
corpus of collaborative experience in practical defence con-
sultations which some would argue ought not to be unduly
disturbed by the creation of yet another organisation in the
same line of business. If a new defence organisation is

16 It has been pointed out to me by my friend Paddy Menaul that there is
already a good deal of defence collaboration in Europe without any of the
corresponding political consensus which I have suggested is a prerequisite
for such co-operation. I would not quarrel with him about the achievements
to date. My argument is not that *no* defence co-operation can take place
without prior agreement on political questions, but that significant developments which are seen to make serious inroads into a state's sovereignty are
unlikely without it.

required it ought, perhaps, to arise out of this evolutionary process which has already acquired the kind of momentum which can be halted only by conscious political decisions.

And there are very real practical difficulties in replacing Europe's rather complicated defence arrangements with a single, coherent system. Undertaking any major structural alterations with a family in residence is inevitably a messy and difficult business. In this particular case, sensible alterations and tidy planning are made even more difficult by awkward relatives. There is, for example, a rich and powerful uncle who has to be accommodated because his continuing support is essential to the family's well-being for a number of years. And there is an even more obstreperous relative who, in any planned refurbishing, has to be provided for even though for the moment he insists on maintaining his own establishment. Equally awkward are those less close relatives who, on common-sense grounds, might more appropriately be accommodated in adjacent cottages but who still insist on remaining under the parental roof.

The very real difficulties of accommodating diverse interests within a single grouping have led some to speculate about the possibility of a defence organisation – perhaps a modified W.E.U. – which was concerned primarily with the problems associated with the Central Front. At least two comments, one general and one specific, are possible. First, it is worth pointing out that effective collaboration in an alliance does not require, as the critics imply, an identity of interests between the members. All that is necessary is that each partner should see an advantage in co-operating. The fact that they do not see the *same* advantage does not matter. Hence, quite diverse states may, for diverse reasons and in the pursuit of diverse interests, co-operate. Second, it is difficult to imagine W.E.U., with its aura of failure, as a revitalised organisation. And from the British point of view, if it was rejuvenated it would be dangerous to assume that Britain could dominate it. On certain plausible growth projections, it may be that by 1980 both France and the Federal Republic will be half as rich again as the United Kingdom. In collaboration with such strong partners the British might find themselves in the back seat.

However, in spite of the difficulties, one may expect the enlargement of the Community to give a further fillip to the integration movement among its members, if only because other international developments are pushing the Europeans in the same direction. And since the enlarged Community includes Britain, France and the Federal Republic – the three most significant military powers in Europe – one might expect their collaborative ventures to be important.

One of the most insistent outside pressures on the Europeans to co-operate in the defence field comes, paradoxically, from the Soviet Union. The residual Soviet threat is sufficiently well appreciated to encourage the West Europeans to improve their co-operative efforts in the security field.[17] In spite of détente, perceptive Europeans have noted that, at the very moment when the United States is tiring of its world role and reducing its overseas involvements, the Soviet Union is becoming interested in playing a global role and is already acquiring the military capability to make it effective. Growing naval strength in the Mediterranean and the continuous, if unspectacular, improvements in Warsaw Pact forces are two clear indications of the way in which the military balance in Europe is shifting against the West. Unfortunately, comparing the military strengths of NATO and the Warsaw Pact is an uncertain business. In 1968, for example, the *Economist* concluded that 'the balance is clearly in Russia's favour even allowing, in one of Mr Healey's favourite phrases, for the political warning time',[18] but Assistant Secretary of Defence, Alain Enthoven, looking at exactly the same data, drew a very different conclusion, 'The comparison . . . certainly does not support the *Economist*'s picture of massive NATO inferiority in conventional forces. On the contrary, an accurate

[17] One commentator on this paper queried the adjective 'residual' as applied to the Soviet threat. By using it I do not mean to imply that the Soviet threat has diminished to the point where it can be regarded as negligible. Indeed, in terms of offensive capability the Soviets are probably more powerful than they have ever been. But in terms of the way in which we interpret their political intentions there is general agreement that they are much less hostile towards Europe than they were in the 1950s. For a more comprehensive analysis of the problem of threat assessment, the reader is referred to an article by the author, 'An Analysis of Threats', *International Relations* (Oct 1971).

[18] *Economist*, 10 Feb 1968.

picture of all the factors indicates rough equality.'[19] Of the two views Mr Healey's has commanded the most general support, and there is now a consensus that, relatively speaking, European military power is being steadily eroded. At the moment it may still be adequate, but there are very real fears that unless positive steps are taken, it will fall below the minimum requirements of deterrence and defence. Duchêne has summarised the position very well:

> Strategically, the Soviet fleets are increasingly impinging on Europe's environment in the Mediterranean and Norwegian seas, as well as, more distantly, the oil routes of the Indian Ocean. On land, Yugoslavia is more concerned about security than at any time since 1948. Economically the U.S.A. is no longer able to guarantee European oil supplies, as in 1956, or the monetary and trading context for growth. And Europe is now beginning to feel a little naked in the winds of the larger world.[20]

So long as the Soviet Union remains ideologically committed to revolutionary change and sufficiently powerful to look as if she might be tempted to try her luck, European states are bound to feel the need to protect themselves. The Soviet threat is real, though more ambiguous than it used to be, and most thoughtful Europeans recognise that the kind of sustained military effort which is required to counter it can most painlessly be achieved on a co-operative, 'European' basis.

Of the numerous political and economic pressures which are encouraging collaboration in the defence field, the most significant is the very real prospect of American withdrawal from the continent they have defended for so long. Of course, President Nixon has emphasised the abiding and undiminished commitment of the United States to defend Western Europe: 'In the third decade of our commitment to Europe, the depth of our relationship is a fact of life. We can no more disengage from Europe than from Alaska.'[21] But the term 'commitment' is ambiguous and can be misleading. In

[19] A. Enthoven, letter to the editor, *Survival*, x 9 (Sep 1968) 308.
[20] Duchêne, 'A New European Defence Community', p. 76.
[21] Richard Nixon, 'U.S. Foreign Policy for the 1970s', a report to the Congress, 18 Feb 1970, p. 20.

the context of American–European relations it may refer either to a legally binding promise by the United States to provide assistance to Western Europe in the event of Soviet aggression, or to an abiding physical peacetime presence in Europe which takes the form of stationing men and equipment in the European theatre. The United States commitment in the former sense is unquestioned, but in the latter sense there is plenty of evidence that it is likely to diminish. Although the Mansfield Resolution was defeated, the mood which it sprang from is likely to remain a vocal and peaceful pressure in American politics. The Nixon Doctrine and the talk about a more genuine partnership and 'burden-sharing' are firm indications that the American military involvement in Europe is likely to change from preponderance to inferiority.

The creation of a Euro-group in NATO, and initiatives such as the European Defence Improvement Programme, may be regarded as the first, tentative European reactions to President Nixon's firm and entirely reasonable insistence that Europe undertake a fair share of its own defence. It seems sensible to suppose that in the face of United States troop withdrawals and a diminution of effort, the Europeans will be forced to make good the deficiencies in their defence posture. However, though the argument is unassailable in logic, it is by no means cast-iron. European politicians may find it politically convenient to believe that if the Americans feel it is safe enough to withdraw, then the threat of Soviet invasion, already fairly incredible to many of them, must be sufficiently near zero for no increased defence effort to be required. Even those who recognise the threat may be tempted to ignore it on the grounds that Western Europe is incapable of dealing with it without crippling herself economically. The argument is that if we in Europe are condemned to living dangerously whatever we do, then we might as well live cheaply as well. In an atmosphere of détente in which every government in Western Europe is trying to reduce its defence expenditure, there are enormous pressures to see it this way. If, however, increased effort is deemed necessary, then increased co-operation in the defence field will seem an attractive way for individual states to minimise their financial burdens. In the end, the very selfish motive of saving money may be the most important pressure towards collaboration, even integration, in the defence field.

There is a depressing intractability about defence economics which may force the states of Europe into reluctant co-operation. The British experience is as relevant as any. At a time when the cost of building a frigate is about 75 per cent higher than it was in the late 1950s, and the capital cost of an armoured regiment equipped with Chieftains about 80 per cent higher than the cost of one equipped with Centurions, the British have reduced the proportion of their G.N.P. spent on defence from about 8 per cent to just over 5 per cent. It seems reasonable to expect that, once inside the Common Market, in order not to be economically disadvantaged, Great Britain will not allow her defence expenditure to exceed the average of her European partners. This would imply that by the end of the decade, and in spite of costs rising more quickly than G.N.P., Britain will be spending less than 4 per cent of her G.N.P. on defence. This is not as much as she – or other European states – can afford, but given the prevailing political climate, it is as much as anyone is prepared to pay.

At this level of effort, it is unlikely that even the larger states of Western Europe will be able to maintain their traditional spectrum of military power. Trying to do too much with too little is a certain recipe for doing nothing effectively. It may be that only by specialising, by deliberately unbalancing their forces, will European states be able to achieve a credible defence posture in any area. If they can co-ordinate their 'unbalancing' policies, West European states might avoid dangerous gaps in their collective defence posture and make significant savings. The argument is that by unbalancing their national forces, the European states will provide properly 'balanced' forces for an entity which is much more powerful than all of them put together. Putting it simply, the Europeans will be able either to maintain existing levels of military strength for less money or improve them for the same amount of money.

This sort of military functionalism presupposes a certain degree of harmony in strategic and tactical doctrine, and a good deal of trust in allies, but as economic pressures mount, it is a pattern of behaviour which European states will find difficult to resist. It should be clear, however, that this kind of specialisation would create very serious personnel problems within the armed forces, and is quite alien to our traditional way of thinking about defence. Moreover, it would be a political hot potato in the sense that participating countries would be consciously and deliberately allocating to their allies full responsibility for important aspects of their own defence. If it happened it would signify a commitment of Europe besides which the present assignment and earmarking of forces to NATO appears quite trivial. Timothy Stanley is probably right in his view that 'it is not in the present political cards to rationalise the division of labour so that one country concentrates on naval forces, another on air forces and so on',[22] but some sort of specialisation is probably inevitable.

There is no need to take the argument to the point where each state provides only one kind of military power. Even some degree of specialisation within the three services would bring considerable benefits. It is quite ridiculous, for example, that a small air force such as the one possessed by the Belgians should attempt the entire spectrum of roles implied by air defence, conventional bombing, nuclear bombing, close support, reconnaissance and anti-submarine. This kind of national diversification which leads even small states to try to do everything is a very inefficient use of resources.

The major argument against specialisation revolves around the possibility that a state may defect from mutually agreed arrangements, thereby leaving its allies exposed and vulnerable in certain categories of weaponry. If, for example, there had been this kind of specialisation within NATO during the first fifteen years of its life, the French withdrawal in 1967 might have had devastating implications for Western security. And in the context of specialisation it may be worth noting that from the British point of view a whole series of commitments outside Europe makes it that much more difficult for the British Government to relinquish certain kinds of capability to her NATO allies.

[22] T. Stanley, 'A Strategic Doctrine for NATO in the 1970s', *Orbis*, xiii, 1 (Spring 1969) 95.

Already, but in a haphazard and therefore dangerous fashion, the smaller European states have found it necessary to specialise. The Belgian Navy, for example, has concentrated on a minesweeping role, and the Norwegian Navy on a coastal role with no deep-sea capability. The Germans have relinquished their nuclear ambitions, and their air force has never attempted to acquire deep penetration capacity. It would be dangerous to read too much into the *ad hoc*, unilaterally decided, specialisation that has gone on so far. After all, there is all the difference in the world between accepting a position of dependence and inadequacy which arises, as it were, out of the natural order of things, and positively organising such a state of affairs by making it official, government policy. Nevertheless, in the long run systematic rationalisation along functional lines may be one way in which Western Europe can maintain a viable defence effort within the budgetary ceilings which are available. These days, money is the key to most decisions in the defence business, and ironically, though a united Europe has been the lofty aspiration of idealists motivated by the noblest sentiments, it may very well turn out that human greed and an obsession with material prosperity are the driving forces which turn aspiration into reality.

The economic advantages and, for those who see it that way, the political advantages of going it with others in the defence field are available across the entire spectrum of weaponry. Not surprisingly, therefore, the pressure upon France and Britain, the only European nuclear powers, to co-operate in nuclear matters is formidable. The financial advantage to both parties would be considerable, and if the joint nuclear force was regarded as the primitive basis of a European deterrent, the political significance is undeniable, although it is debatable whether an Anglo-French force 'held in trust' would help unify Europe or whether it would create a nuclear elite which would divide Europe.

The problems of going it alone can be put quite simply. In the case of the French, the acquisition of nuclear capacity, even nuclear capacity of dubious effectiveness, is imposing a very heavy burden on the defence budget, and as Soviet defence systems become more sophisticated, it is unlikely that the French effort will diminish. During the third military plan from 1971 to 1975 it is estimated that one-third of the £7,200 million to be spent on weapon procurement will be for nuclear arms.[23] Already the French spend more on their strategic forces than on any of the three services. The 1972 defence budget allocates £372 million or 27.5 per cent of the total to the nuclear deterrent.[24] It is possible that this figure will reduce to about 20 per cent by 1975, but this will be about ten times the British figure at that time.[25] As Ian Smart says, France is facing a great and increasing economic burden, the scale of which threatens to force the French Government to choose whether to increase its defence budget as a whole or to persist in penalising programmes for the re-equipment of the armed forces with modern conventional weapons.[26]

In the case of Britain, where the problem is one of perpetuating the usefulness of ageing systems and, in the long run, of replacing them with a new generation of weaponry, the financial burden is not so immediately onerous, but it is likely to increase very sharply indeed if Britain wishes to retain a viable deterrent in the 1980s and beyond. Hardening warheads and fitting M.I.R.V.s is an expensive business, and if the British decide to move to the next generation of delivery vehicles – probably U.L.M.S. – the costs will be astronomical. On balance it would seem that, of the two states, France is the more likely to be able to pursue an independent nuclear policy in the long run, but even she may fail in the end.

The choices available to both states are limited. Each can either co-operate with the United States, continue independently, co-operate with each other, or allow the present forces to 'rust out' without replacement. The French are unlikely to give up or to co-operate with the United States. The British, though they may go it alone in the short run, are quite likely to give up if they cannot co-operate with either the United States or France, or, ideally, both. For all sorts of reasons,

[23] *Financial Times*, 30 July 1970, quoting M. Debré. (In these figures an exchange rate of £1 = F13.5 is used.)

[24] D. Lewardowski, 'National Defence Budget 1972', *Revue de Défense Nationale* (Jan 1972) p. 26.

[25] I. Smart, *Future Conditional: The Prospects for Anglo-French Nuclear Co-operation*, Adelphi Paper No. 78 (London: International Institute for Strategic Studies, 1971) p. 20.   [26] Ibid.

political, technical and economic, some kind of Anglo-French co-operation seems desirable, but the obstacles are very real. Co-operation is hampered by British integration in NATO, by the nuclear relationship between Britain and the United States and the restrictive policies inherent in that association, by the suspicions and uneasiness of the Soviet Union, the United States and some European states, and, not least, by the Gaullist philosophy which, though crumbling around the edges, still dominates French policy. And there are very large question marks over the *kind* of co-operation which is possible. The French appear to want mainly technical and economic co-operation which would enable them to improve their own forces. They are very hostile to ideas of co-operation in any operational sense and seek mainly to promote national ambitions through collective effort. The British too are aware of the advantages of independent control, but the government tends to place more emphasis on the political, 'Europe-building' role of co-operative effort.

Ideally, nuclear co-operation should follow rather than precede political integration, but time may not permit this. Military capability takes years to acquire, and unless co-operation is initiated in the near future, neither Britain, nor France, nor Europe will have any strategic nuclear forces after the present generation of weapons. The technologies involved in the nuclear weapons industry are so sophisticated that, once halted, it is doubtful if they could be picked up again even by a politically united Europe. The protracted timetable of weapon developments imparts a very special urgency to the question of Anglo-French nuclear co-operation, but there can be no confidence that the states involved will be able to overcome the difficulties. The expansion of the European Economic Community to include the United Kingdom has naturally provoked a good deal of discussion about Anglo-French nuclear co-operation; but it is worth remembering that although continued French opposition to British entry would have made such co-operation unthinkable, the withdrawal of that opposition does not make it plausible. Fundamentally, the problems of nuclear co-operation have very little to do with the development of the Community except in the most general sense, and it would therefore be unrealistic to suppose that, as a result of British entry, progress will be suddenly easier.

Pressure to co-operate in the defence field is but one example of a wider kind of economic pressure which is forcing the European states to join forces in a variety of technological fields. Already in Europe there is a general awareness of the problems which confront medium-range powers competing in technologically sophisticated fields with the United States. The economic and technological gap has been well documented by such writers as Jean-Jacques Servan-Schreiber and Christopher Layton, who have pointed out some of the implications which follow from the fact that in such future-oriented industries as telecommunications, aerospace, computers and electronics, the United States has built up a convincing and increasing lead.[27] De Gaulle's accusation of 'economic imperialism' and Mr Wilson's fear of 'industrial helotry' both have their origins in the serious imbalance between European and American technology. European defence industries in particular have been seriously weakened by American competition. The extent of the problem facing European governments and defence industries can be deduced from the following crude statistics. In 1965 West European countries spent rather more than one-third as much on defence as the United States, that is to say, $22,000 million as against $53,000 million. The average annual military R. & D. expenditure of Britain, France and Germany between 1955 and 1965 was about one-tenth that of the United States.

As a result of her enormous defence expenditure, the United States is able to produce more sophisticated weapons over a wider range than her European competitors. What is more, since the United States armed services provide a much bigger home market than is available to any single European state, the unit cost of United States weapons invariably works out cheaper than that of any European counterpart. And because of the high quality of American management, United States weapons usually have a shorter development time than

---

[27] See J.-J. Servan-Schreiber, *The American Challenge* (London: Hamish Hamilton 1968); C. Layton, *European Advanced Technology: A Programme for Integration* (London: Allen & Unwin, 1969).

comparable European systems, as Alastair Buchan has pointed out:

> . . . the dilemma that haunts any European government which commits R. & D. funds to a defence project is that it may get a certain distance, find a broadly equivalent American project being developed at greater speed, and discover that its European neighbours who have not committed R. & D. funds would rather buy the cheaper American product, so that the eventual market for its own will be small and will thus have an eventual high unit cost.[28]

The problems facing the European arms industry are exacerbated by at least three other hard facts of life. First, at a time when all West European governments are trying to hold, if not reduce, their present level of defence expenditure, the cost of developing and producing weapons is increasing. Second, since Western Europe faces a sophisticated enemy in competition with the United States, the speed with which complex equipment becomes obsolescent is likely to be quite fast. Third, the United States pursues a very aggressive sales policy in the European market.

Perhaps there is no answer to the problems which face European states bent on maintaining viable national defence industries in the face of American competition, but it is possible that even if they cannot survive individually, the defence industries of European states could live to enjoy moderate prosperity if they would learn to pool their resources systematically. At the moment, the West Europeans waste their resources on maintaining separate national armies, defence ministries, R. & D. establishments, etc. They further complicate their planning and diminish their funds by senselessly duplicating the production of arms and equipment which differ in design, requirements, manufacturing standards and performance. Organised and widespread co-operation, let alone integration, instead of purely national procurement policies, would certainly result in the better use of money, streamlined industries and a bigger market. The advantages

[28] A. Buchan, 'The Implications of a European System for Defence Technology', in *The United States and Europe: Defence, Technology and the Western Alliance* (London: Institute for Strategic Studies, 1967) p. 4.

of centralised management and spending within a big market are incontestable, and the Europeans have already taken tentative steps towards collaboration in the defence field. The Plowden Report emphasised the point in the aerospace field, and such projects as Jaguar reflect the kind of co-operation which is being attempted.

At the moment a number of joint projects are in progress. Besides the Jaguar close support and attack aircraft, there are Anglo-French programmes for helicopters and missiles – Martel and Exocet. There is German, Italian and British collaboration in the development and production of artillery systems, and Belgium has joined Britain in the production of light armoured vehicles. The next ambitious project, of course, is the multi-role combat aircraft (M.R.C.A.) which involves the United Kingdom, Germany and Italy in the formation of an international company, Panavia, which is responsible for the design, development, production and marketing of the plane. Air Vice-Marshal Menaul has suggested that 'the Panavia organisation could become the basic organisation for the production of future European air weapons systems'.[29]

However, whether this kind of relatively modest co-operation is sufficient is a moot point. There are many down-to-earth realists who argue, very persuasively, that given a politically divided Europe in which nationalist aspirations continue to be important, little steps are the only ones which are feasible and have any chance of succeeding. W. Schütze has suggested that *ad hoc* co-operation in specific joint procurement ventures and progress towards a common logistic system and deployment in the European area is about as much as can be reasonably hoped for.[30] On the other hand, there are some who believe that these modest co-operative ventures are woefully inadequate. René Foch has condemned them utterly:

> Today, technological Europe is a cemetery of lost illusions, commemorating the failure of a series of chimerical

[29] S. W. B. Menaul, 'Britain in Europe: The Defence Aspect', *Defence*, II, 9 (Sep 1971) 29.
[30] W. Schütze, *European Defence Co-operation and NATO* (Paris: Atlantic Institute, 1969).

national ambitions and ill-conceived plans for international co-operation. The reasons are clear enough: sectorial institutions paralysed by the obsession of a 'fair return', precarious budgets undergoing constant review, methods of management which have more in common with the Congress of Vienna than the Harvard Business School.[31]

Others have been equally sceptical of the kind of *ad hoc* co-operative ventures which have so far been attempted. John Calmann, commenting on Anglo-French co-operation, reached the conclusion that the aim of both states was 'to retain a free hand while playing at integration in the limited sector of the aircraft industry'.[32] In a related study on weapon standardisation and the problems of common production of weapons, Robert Rhodes James has made a similar point. He quotes with approval a statement of General Vanderantor, that 'the individual NATO nation does not want international agencies dabbling in its own procurement business and feels capable of selecting its own equipment. It wants, instead, a means of persuading the other nations to buy that very equipment.'[33]

Foch is convinced that the method of occasional co-operation without an overall plan is bound to fail. He therefore favours the creation of genuinely European institutions to organise technological co-operation on a Community basis. In the defence field he suggests a European Armaments Agency to define the needs of European countries for new armaments and to organise and finance the necessary research, development and industrial production for the equipment of European defence – at least in the conventional field.[34] This proposal is not very different from Alastair Buchan's idea of 'A European Advanced Project Authority designed to assure a Europe-wide market for expensive defence products by getting prior agreement on requirements, by spreading the cost of research, and by organising development and production wherever the most effective

[31] R. Foch, *Europe and Technology* (Paris: Atlantic Institute, 1970) p. 52.
[32] John Calmann, 'European Co-operation in Defence Technology: The Political Aspect', in *Defence, Technology and the Western Alliance*, p. 11.
[33] Robert Rhodes James, 'Standardisation and Common Production of Weapons in NATO', ibid., p. 22.
[34] Foch, *Europe and Technology*, p. 48.

facilities exist'.[35] And it also has something in common with Duchêne's notion of a European Defence Support Organisation with an interest in procurement, training and logistics.[36] Already there are clear signs that NATO politicians are moving in this direction. European defence ministers have recently resolved that consultation and collaboration should in future characterise the procurement of NATO weapons. And preliminary discussions have already started between Britain and Germany on the kind of tank that NATO will require as a replacement for the Chieftain and the Leopard.[37]

The pressures towards defence co-operation and integration in Western Europe are increasing, and the advantages to be had from it are real and valuable. But it would be dangerous to conclude that progress was inevitable. After all, the incentives to co-operate have been acknowledged for many years but so far have had singularly little effect. For all the talk about joint procurement, standardised weaponry and spare parts, integrated logistics, etc., the record is depressingly thin. Few would argue that in the coming years progress is likely to be rapid, but it may very well be less slow and painful than hitherto. There are some indications that the Common Market countries, by virtue of their co-operative experience, have learned to overcome some of the teething problems which beset joint enterprises. And the Europe of 1972 is quite different from the one that accepted the failure of the first European Defence Community. The problems faced by medium-sized powers trying to maintain independent yet viable forces against a sophisticated super-power enemy are more keenly appreciated, and the pressures to join forces are more relentless.

[35] Buchan, 'The Implications of a European System for Defence Technology', in *Defence, Technology and the Western Alliance*, p. 19.

[36] Duchêne, 'A New European Defence Community', p. 80.

[37] See 'A Melting Pot Approach for Europe's Costly Armaments', *The Times*, 14 July 1972.

5
Prospects for European Arms Co-operation

HUGH GREEN*

This paper deals with the prospects for European arms co-operation. It is common knowledge that the problems of defence finance are aggravated by the steadily increasing cost and complexity of modern weapons. The cost of both development and production is increasing, and because fewer weapons can be afforded the smaller production runs drive the unit costs of production still higher. The European countries therefore have an obvious interest in finding ways of reducing development costs and securing the advantages of long production runs. This process is loosely described as collaboration, but it is important to realise that there are a number of different forms of common procurement.

Collaboration on individual projects is the method that comes most easily to mind. Carrying out a development programme in collaboration tends to add to the total cost because of the need for liaison between the partners, cross-checking of work, extra prototypes and so on. It is impossible to demonstrate exactly the ratio in which development cost increases, because the difference must vary from project to project and it will never be possible to compare historically the cost of a project carried out in isolation with the cost of the same project carried out internationally. Experience with the Jaguar, however, suggests that with this type of aircraft the extra cost of splitting the programme between two partners is of the order of 20 per cent. But even with this increase the cost to each partner is only 60 per cent of what it would

* Assistant Under-Secretary (Operational Requirements), Ministry of Defence, London

have cost them to carry out the programme alone. Sharing a development project among more than three partners tends to increase its complexity significantly, with consequent effects on both time and cost. Since there are more partners the cost to each will not rise proportionately, but the extra time and greater risk make this type of project vulnerable.

Collaboration on production need not be preceded by collaboration in development, since a collaborative production programme can embrace partners who have taken no part in design or development and whose contribution to development costs could well be confined to royalty payments. In collaborative production programmes it is usual for each partner to carry out final assembly in its own territory, but the benefits of long production runs can be secured by what is called single-point procurement. This means that total production of each common component is carried out at a single point of manufacture: the sharing of work between the partners is secured by allocation between them of the different components. Again it is very difficult to calculate the difference in unit cost between this method of production and production on a purely national basis. Experience suggests that for the Jaguar type of programme the differential, quantity for quantity, is of the order of 10 per cent, but the application of the learning curve to the combined production quantity (for each doubling of the quantity the unit cost falls to 80 per cent) more than offsets this addition.

Collaboration on individual projects is not the only way to overcome the problem of rising development and production costs. The sale abroad of equipment developed nationally provides a contribution (though a delayed one) to development costs through the levies paid by exporting manufacturers or through the element in the selling price to direct customers which is attributable to development. Exports are also a valuable means of increasing total production and thus reducing unit cost. For national projects, these benefits accrue in their entirety to the country responsible for the project. Exports can also increase the market for collaborative projects beyond the size which collaboration itself ensures, but the contribution to development costs – and the balance-of-payment benefits – have to be shared between the partners rather than retained in total by a single country.

The converse of this method, but still a way of reducing the cost of defence procurement, is to buy equipment abroad. In doing this it is necessary to consider the consequences for domestic industry and the balance-of-payments effects, but in purely financial terms buying abroad (particularly from the United States, the production source with the biggest assured domestic market) may sometimes be cheaper than either national development or collaboration. Certainly for equipments for which the national requirement is small, particularly if development costs are high, purchase abroad may well be the optimum course.

There is a fourth method of procurement which might be described as reciprocal procurement and which in a sense combines the second and third of the methods described previously. This is where countries share two or more projects in a way which allows responsibility for the development of each project (and, if desired, its production as well) to rest wholly with a single country. In this way, for the group of projects as a whole, the savings through sharing the cost of development are not offset by any increase in the total cost of development and the full benefits of maximising production runs can be secured. Moreover, the efficiency with which individual projects are managed is not eroded by division of responsibility. For this method to be acceptable, however, there must be a broad balance between the components of the package in their timing, their cost and their technological content. It is not easy to find a group of projects in a programme which meets this criterion; and the firm or industry which succeeds in winning one part of a reciprocal programme does so at the expense of another firm or industry which has to forgo any share in the other part. The difficulty of balancing such a large project as the multi-role combat aircraft (M.R.C.A.) makes it virtually inevitable that projects on this scale will be carried out on a collaborative basis.

A further argument for sharing development programmes through the various methods described and arranging common production programmes is that it leads to greater standardisation of equipment among the participating countries. Significant advantages can of course be obtained without there being complete commonality of equipment. For example:

(a) In communications, common parameters or even interface equipment may well be sufficient to achieve the necessary interoperability rather than complete standardisation.

(b) Standard fuels and standard procedures may be sufficient to secure the cross-operation of aircraft.

(c) Common ballistic parameters permit ammunition not otherwise standard to be fired from artillery which equally is not otherwise standard.

(d) The use of common components (e.g. tank tracks, engine components) permits a measure of logistic flexibility even in the absence of complete standardisation.

There are areas indeed where diversity of equipment offers positive operational advantages in the sense that it increases the spread of capability which the enemy has to cover. This is true of radars, electronic counter-measures and guidance frequencies. Nevertheless, there are obvious ways in which the use of completely standardised equipment improves interoperability, operational flexibility and the flexibility of logistic support. These military advantages are coming to be recognised with growing clarity and are reinforcing the economic arguments for common procurement.

Equipment collaboration is increasingly seen by European governments as one means of making better use of the limited resources which they can devote to defence and of developing a more coherent approach to European defence. Progress in this field is becoming a touchstone of the readiness of countries to move towards a more distinctly European stance on defence matters. Political will is not a *deus ex machina* which can be called on to override practical considerations regardless of their strength, but given the powerful arguments which point towards a greater degree of collaboration, the political impetus will certainly carry weight.

The advantages of common equipment as described above

are not a recently revealed truth; on the contrary, they have attracted procurement planners for many years. They are undoubtedly difficult to secure, but they have influenced procurement planning within Europe to an extent which is not always fully recognised. Consider, for instance, the main features of current European defence procurement policies.

(a) The smaller countries have gone a long way towards solving their procurement finance problems by the method described earlier, namely by buying abroad. To a large extent they buy from the United States, but not a little of their equipment comes from France and the United Kingdom. None of these countries spends very much on R. & D.; in effect they make use of other countries' R. & D. at the cheapest level through their purchases abroad. Some of them develop an occasional project on a government basis, but more as a means of keeping their scientific staff up to date and better able to discharge their main role of advising on weapons from other sources. To some extent also equipments are developed by individual firms as private ventures. There are undoubtedly areas of technological expertise among these smaller countries, but they spend much of their defence scientific effort on assessment, with little to spare for national or collaborative development. Even where attempts are made to increase development effort, for example in aerospace and electronics, these countries appear to be content in many procurement areas to wait to see how United States and European developments compare and to make a choice only when these projects have entered production. To ask these countries to take part in European collaborative development on a markedly increased scale would have the effect of increasing the amount of money they had to spend on defence procurement and of bringing this expenditure forward in time. If it is assumed that the European countries will not spend more than they now do on defence, other parts of their programmes would suffer and their overall capability would be reduced.

(b) The Germans are taking seriously the increase of their development capability, through both national and collaborative programmes, in aerospace, guided weapons, electronics, ordnance and armour. But as off-set for the foreign exchange cost of American troops in Germany they have hitherto procured a large proportion of their equipment from the United States and it seems likely that this will continue to influence their procurement policies.

(c) This leaves the French, who are very similar to ourselves in terms of development and production capability in a wide range of technologies. The French attach great importance to their defence-related industries; they see in them a powerful means of establishing national strength and they support them with military projects optimised so far as possible towards meeting export requirements, which often seem to take precedence over the requirements of the French Services themselves. The French are, however, as alert as anyone to the economic pressures on defence procurement and have embarked on extensive collaborative programmes. But their approach is characterised by objective calculation of their national interests and they are at pains to preserve an acceptable degree of French leadership in the collaborative projects which they undertake. Indeed, their preference is against sharing management responsibility for individual projects and towards the reciprocal procurement type of arrangement. If they succeed in taking the lead in a particular area (of their success with Exocet), their negotiating position for setting up a reciprocal procurement arrangement is that much the stronger.

Against this background, our own procurement policy has been a flexible one. We have maintained a large national R. & D. programme not only in our efforts to provide the forces with cost-effective equipment but to preserve our industrial base and to exploit the export potential of successful projects. By no means all projects can be 'winners', but projects such as Rapier and Harrier have clearly made an impact on world markets and their potential for exports in the long run is very considerable. At the same time we are not averse to buying abroad where equipment is clearly beyond our capability (e.g. Polaris), where requirements are small and national development would be uneconomical (e.g. plans, now abandoned through budgetary pressure, to buy medium-lift helicopters from the United States), or where industry, not necessarily through its own fault, cannot meet our requirements. In a number of key equipment areas, how-ever, we have been pursuing collaboration as the most eco-nomical form of procurement which does not damage our industrial base or create balance-of-payment problems. Ever since the collapse in the early 1960s of the attempts to estab-lish common procurement on the basis of NATO Basic Military Requirements (N.B.M.R.s), we have devoted great efforts, both through the NATO machinery and through our bilateral contacts with most of the West European countries, to identify projects suitable for collaboration and to translate these into actual collaborative programmes. The record is not unimpressive and the process is a continuing one.

The list below illustrates the extent to which collaboration has established itself in our procurement policy and the basis which now exists for extending it further.

M.R.C.A. For the R.A.F., this is its most important future project. Development is shared between the United King-dom, West Germany and Italy. Although each country will assemble its aircraft, production will be by single-point procurement.

Jaguar. This is being developed to meet both French and British requirements for a trainer and a close support aircraft and the French requirement for a carrier-borne attack aircraft. Development and production are shared between the two countries, the latter on single-point procure-ment.

Anglo-French helicopters. This collaborative programme represents a form of reciprocal procurement in that the French are responsible for designing two of the helicopters and the United Kingdom the third. To balance out the work, however, the partner country in each case undertakes development sub-contracts and production is on the usual dual-assembly single-point procurement basis.

Martel. This is a dual-purpose missile (anti-radar and TV-guided), with France developing the anti-radar head and the United Kingdom the TV head and the development of common parts divided between the two.

Exocet. This naval surface-to-surface missile has been developed by France, but a proportion of the components is being produced in the United Kingdom.

F.H. 70, S.P. 70 and R.S. 80. These projects are a towed 155-mm gun, a self-propelled 155-mm gun, and a free-flight rocket system respectively. The development of F.H. 70, which is already well advanced, is shared between West Germany and the United Kingdom with each country responsible for some of the components. Italy has joined the project too late to join in development, but will have a share in production which will be by single-point procurement. The other two projects are at an earlier stage, but it is intended that development and production should be shared between all three countries with the United Kingdom responsible for co-ordination. These three projects offer the prospect of creating a West European-wide family of artillery/rocket systems.

Combat vehicle reconnaissance (tracked) (C.V.R.(T)). This vehicle, in a number of different versions, has been developed by the United Kingdom, but Belgium has now been associated with the programme through placing an order for 700 vehicles. In return for a contribution to R. & D. costs, production will be shared with Belgian industry both for the combined British–Belgian requirements and for exports. Again there are prospects of creating a European family of light armoured vehicles.

Given the development cycle of modern equipment (up to ten years for major complex weapons) and its life in service (perhaps ten years for weapons whose technology is advancing fast and rather longer for the less sophisticated types), the rate at which new collaborative projects can be launched is obviously limited. Nevertheless, there are a number of projects whose development will need to be launched in the next two or three years which are natural candidates for collaboration and where the necessary conditions for collaboration will be thoroughly explored. These include the next generation of medium-altitude surface-to-air guided weapons, the next-generation main battle tank and the Jaguar/Harrier successor. Moreover, we can have reasonable confidence that when the need for replacing the present collaborative projects arrives, they too will be handled on a collaborative basis.

Although, as the previous paragraphs have demonstrated, the United Kingdom has not been idle in Europe in promoting equipment collaboration, the question is being increasingly asked, and at the highest levels, what more can be done and what contribution can such further effort make towards improving the relative effectiveness of Western defence. The options fall into two broad groups; measures of obligatory co-operation and measures of voluntary co-operation. Before these are analysed and compared, it might be useful to comment briefly on the main obstacles which, at present, collaboration has to face and to make some comments on the costs of collaboration and its implications for European industry.

Given the undoubted advantages of collaboration, it is helpful to consider briefly the factors which have inhibited progress. The following are some of the main considerations:

(a) The alternatives of pursuing national developments and relying on exports to reduce costs, or of straight purchase from the cheapest market also have their attractions and, depending on the circumstances, may well represent more valid options than collaboration.

(b) Production of common equipment demands exact agreement between the partners on equipment characteristics and on the date of introduction into service. It also demands readiness to bear the costs. Equipment characteristics stem from operational requirements which in turn depend on tactical concepts and strategic philosophies. These are matters on which professional opinion can legitimately differ widely and is rarely constant. Differing traditions of professional thought or differing attitudes to the role of one's country in European combat cannot be reconciled quickly. Differences of national wealth influence the level of equipment cost and effectiveness which countries can afford and the rate at which equipment can be replaced. A country which can afford relatively sophisticated forces may find it more economical to adopt expensive but multi-role equipment. A smaller country may have to make do with comparatively simple and cheap equipment (cf. the attitude of the Dutch and Belgians to the M.R.C.A.). The smaller countries can afford to re-equip less frequently than their wealthier partners either can or (in the collective interest) should. These are economic factors which run counter to collaboration and tend to strengthen the seller–buyer mode of procurement.

(c) The other main obstacle to collaboration is industrial. So long as countries set great store by their individual industrial and technological strength and recognise the very significant contribution which defence procurement can make to it, so long will they be chary of schemes for collaboration which change to their disadvantage the relative position between them and others. A significant change in the pattern of European industry in the direction of international association will be necessary before these fears can be overcome.

Various attempts have been made to measure the costs of collaboration through comparing the costs of alternative ways of procuring typical future projects. Nothing very new has emerged from these studies, but they serve to confirm the conclusions which have encouraged collaboration in the past. Collaboration between a smaller number of partners in the development of major complex projects undoubtedly saves money for each partner in spite of the extra costs of collaboration. The cheapest method of all is for one country to carry out development on behalf of the others, but, as explained earlier, the acceptability of this depends on the scope for reciprocity. As regards production, the aggregation of individual requirements into a common production line allows economies of scale which, provided requirements are large enough, more than offset the costs of collaboration. Again the cheapest method of all is for one country to produce the total requirement, but again this ignores the problem of reciprocity.

It is also necessary to consider the likely trends in the relationship between future defence demands and future capacity in the defence-related industries of Western Europe, to see to what extent military demand is essential to the survival of these industries. In most industries defence is not the dominant customer and it cannot be said that without defence demand these industries will die. But the demand for high standards in military equipment is a stimulus to innovation and a significant factor in maintaining the health of advanced-technology industries. To the extent that collaboration enables procurement to be carried out economically within Europe in areas where purely national programmes could not be sustained, it helps to preserve and develop a European technological base. In the aerospace industry military demand represents a large proportion of the whole. But in the civil and in the military fields, some form of European association of firms is essential if they are to continue to be able to compete with America.

There are a number of ways in which European governments might accept an obligation to co-operate in defence procurement and introduce inducements and constraints to promote its implementation. There are two main options to be considered:

(a) Creation of a European common market in defence equipment, with inducements for collaboration in procurement and constraints to discharge offshore purchase.

(b) Creation of an autonomous European Defence Procurement Agency responsible to European ministers for taking the initiative in promoting common procurement.

The object of a defence common market would be to create an assured market for European defence industries and one that was equitably balanced between all its members. Protection could be secured by discrimination against outside

buyers; to achieve a more equitable balance, the right to
discriminate against the partners could be restricted. Protection need not be so high as to remove all incentive to
efficiency, and within the protected market there could be an
element of competition. The less developed countries could
be given incentives to remain members of the market. The
principal features of such a scheme, once the range of equipment to be covered had been defined, might include the
payment of substantial levies by members on any purchases
from outside the market; similar levies would be paid on
equipment purchased from their own nationals. The proceeds
of both levies would be used to provide bonuses to governments buying defence equipment from other market members.

The operation of these rules would, hopefully, protect the
market and force members to rely to a greater extent than
now on each other's industrial efforts. This would make it
easier to agree on common equipment designs; and the
growth of international consortia and the economical sharing
of development and production might be encouraged.

Although such a scheme has certain theoretical attractions,
it ignores the realities of the present industrial pattern with
respect both to the United States and to the distribution of
technological strength in Europe. Discrimination against the
United States would be counter-productive for a number of
reasons:

(a) There is pressure on the Germans to use their offset
foreign exchange to buy United States equipment.

(b) We derive a great deal of basic research information
from the United States, which it would be prohibitively
expensive to generate on our own.

(c) United States competition, potential if not actual, is a
powerful stimulus to the efficiency of European firms.
A closed European market would remove this spur.

(d) Procurement options are a necessary safeguard against
the failure of particular projects, and United States
industry could be a useful long-stop.

(e) For highly sophisticated equipment such as Polaris, or
equipment for which we need relatively small quanti-

ties, the United States may well be the only sensible procurement source.

(f) Discrimination against defence purchases from the United States might attract counter-discrimination against European exports, not only in the immediate defence field but in related industries such as aerospace.

As regards the pattern within Europe, a scheme on the lines proposed could operate successfully only if defence technology were distributed within Europe much more evenly than it actually is. France is the only country with a broad-based defence technological capability comparable with our own. The Germans' capability rests on a rather narrower base, and their participation in projects such as the M.R.C.A. represents an attempt to widen it into more advanced technologies. The rest of the West European countries have narrower defence capabilities still. The rationalisation of European defence technology ought to lead to a trimming of effort in each of the countries concerned, but the United Kingdom would not wish to see its relative position seriously eroded. The trouble with schemes for financial incentives and constraints on the lines proposed is that they are relatively crude and insensitive and do not distinguish between projects ripe for collaboration and those not. The smaller European countries would no doubt welcome these opportunities to broaden their capabilities at the expense of their bigger partners, but there would be a serious risk that technological growth in the smaller countries would be stimulated at a faster rate than could be managed, with serious consequences for European procurement. Members of a defence common market would also wish to control the pace and volume of the transfer of technology to competitors, particularly at a time when the general environment of the E.E.C. will be one of increased competition. It seems inconsistent with present French policy that they should accept this sort of restriction on their technological growth. So far as United Kingdom industry is concerned, the concept of imposing levies on national production and subsidising imports would be difficult to commend. Common market techniques may be effective as a regulator of a system which is already in reasonable balance, but they might carry serious dangers for the United Kingdom's industrial and technological position in Western Europe as we know it.

Another possible approach to common procurement would be to place in the hands of some centralised authority the responsibility for defining the specifications for European equipment and for supervising their execution. The basis for such an arrangement might be an inter-governmental undertaking to co-operate in the progressive standardisation of military equipment. The responsibility for proposing standardised specifications might rest with an autonomous international agency with its own staff. The agency would attempt to reconcile differing national specifications but would not be bound by national views. These agency-sponsored specifications might be put to countries collectively (perhaps at ministerial level) for approval as standard specifications. Production of non-standard equipment need not be forbidden but could be discouraged by financial penalties. As regards common procurement, the agency would be responsible for letting contracts and would be reimbursed by customer countries. Contracts could either be allocated among member countries who had agreed to produce a given item of standard equipment, or reliance could be placed on straight competition among commercial firms. The object of such a scheme would be to secure the military advantages of standardising equipment as well as the economies of scale to be expected from common procurement. The establishment of an international agency might be expected to have some political impact and to be seen as giving some practical expression to the idea of a common European defence effort.

Again, despite its theoretical attractions, such a scheme has to be judged from a proper understanding of the complexities of defence procurement. The following are among the more important points to bear in mind:

(a) Agreement on detailed characteristics of military equipment presupposes agreement on the broad tasks it has to perform within an agreed strategic framework and on the concepts for its tactical use. Unless a European-wide agreement has already been reached on this framework, an autonomous agency is in no position to put its own proposals in a valid context and there is no alternative but for the user countries to reach their own agreement on these questions.

(b) Equipment planning cannot be divorced from the rest of military planning. Equipment characteristics depend on logistic and maintenance philosophy and training philosophy as well as on direct military requirements. Until a collective European view has been formed on these matters (a very long-term prospect indeed), there is a danger that military equipment designed by fiat will prove difficult to operate and costly to maintain.

(c) Equipment characteristics are also very closely influenced by what the user countries can afford. Unless the agency had common funds at its disposal (and there is no prospect in the foreseeable future that the principle of national financial responsibility for equipment will be breached), it would have no budgetary framework to which to relate its proposals.

(d) The mutual adjustment between the characteristics that the military authorities would like to secure and the technical options available for meeting them is a painstaking process which demands immense expertise from both the military and the scientific sides. Scientific establishments with large numbers of highly qualified and experienced staff are necessary. The creation of an autonomous agency with its own expert staff, either alongside or in place of existing national staff, would be an extremely difficult and long-drawn-out task.

(e) The complexities of reaching agreement on the various operational technological and industrial factors involved make it very difficult to carry out collaborative development successfully within a group of more than two or three partners.

There are therefore some severe practical objections to the setting-up of a European Arms Procurement Agency. In addition it is questionable whether this step would have any positive political impact. Since we are dealing with equipment whose gestation period may be as much as ten years and where life in service may be even longer, we cannot expect rapid changes to come about. The next generation of tanks, even if they are European, will not appear until 1980. It is difficult to keep an area like this in the public eye. Indeed, if the impression is created by the setting-up of new institutions that a new era has been introduced, it will only be a matter of time before the inevitably slow tempo of events will create a reaction of disillusion.

In general, these radical schemes for enforcing equipment collaboration represent a leap forward beyond the capacity of the countries concerned to absorb fundamental changes in the way in which weapons are procured, even if some of the principles underlying these schemes were less questionable. It is essential to preserve continuity in the weapon supply system, yet there is a real risk that changes of the sort represented by these options would lead to inordinate delays in the settling of operational requirements and create a fair degree of confusion on the European industrial front. The consequences for the re-equipping of our forces could be serious.

There are two other options which might be described as obligatory co-operation, though they fall short of the schemes so far considered. These are:

(a) Undertakings (which might initially be confined to certain countries and categories of equipment) not to initiate any procurement except on the basis of a collaborative venture.

(b) Agreement to give preference in defence procurement to transnational European consortia.

Again, the difficulty is that undertakings in this form are too blunt and insensitive to suit the many different situations with which we may be faced. As regards (a), the difficulty is that such an undertaking would be binding (or could only be broken with grave embarrassment) in circumstances which proved unpropitious for collaboration and which could not necessarily be foreseen. A whole complex of considerations has to be satisfied before a collaborative project can move to a successful conclusion, by no means all of which are apparent at the start. To enter commitments without a full understanding of their implications can be risky.

Similar objections can be raised against (b). Transnational consortia obviously will be in a favourable position, other things being equal, to secure participation in collaborative projects. However, consortia can vary in the depth of their integration from shell companies with little substance to genuine mergers. A blanket assurance to give consortia preference might not necessarily work to Britain's advantage.

The alternative to obligatory co-operation is to continue with the present permissive, or voluntary, approach to collaboration in which countries remain free to seek partners where they can find them. What are the prospects here? The situation has in fact changed quite considerably over the last year or so, mainly as a result of the attention which European ministers have given to the subject, and the prospects for extending equipment collaboration within Europe are now rather brighter than they were:

(a) The most significant development has been the agreement reached in the summer of 1972 between Euro-group ministers on a set of principles for equipment collaboration, the governing theme of which is the avoidance of unnecessary duplication. Countries undertake to keep each other informed on the timing and content of plans for future military equipment, either through existing NATO machinery or through *ad hoc* arrangements. The object is to identify areas where collaboration seems especially important or promising. When any Euro-group country is preparing or drafting a military planning requirement for any item of equipment which could offer significant prospects for collaboration, it will ascertain from the other countries whether they have the same or similar intentions and whether they have initiated a development on the basis of a relevant existing requirement. The planned characteristics of the equipment will not be finalised until the country has satisfied itself that any substantial possibilities of harmonisation have been explored. Once the general possibility of a common need has been recognised, efforts will be made first to harmonise equipment characteristics and second to agree how the equipment should be jointly provided. Ministers have recognised that no single pattern of joint procurement can be laid down as standard. Depending on circumstances, the right course might be joint development, joint production, manufacture under licence, straightforward purchase, or a combination of methods.

(b) In agreeing these principles, ministers have identified a number of areas to which member countries should give priority in their planning, as offering the best prospects for collaboration, and the Euro-group National Armaments Directors will keep these projects under review. It is recognised that the guidelines are no more than an instrument; they cannot alone generate actual collaborative projects. Practical results will still require personal attention and strong direction by ministers themselves, and a determination to accept flexibility in the assessment of national needs in order to achieve the wider advantages of joint action. Perhaps the most significant feature of this new development is that henceforth countries will not be able to pursue unjustifiable unilateral policies without running the gauntlet of scrutiny by their allies at the highest level.

(c) The need to work within a Euro-group framework will give added impetus to the policies that have hitherto been followed. The general philosophy has already been to encourage as wide an exchange of information about future equipment plans as possible, both through the NATO complex of committees and through bilateral contacts, so that potential partners can identify in good time the possibilities for collaboration and pursue them as appropriate. In this way countries can relate their collaboration equipment planning to the rest of their defence planning and can make balanced judgements, without the constraints of artificially induced distortions, on all the relevant operational technological and industrial factors involved.

So far as Britain is concerned, there is no risk that realistic options for collaboration will be overlooked or not pursued vigorously. The pressures on the defence budget are very considerable indeed and our self-interest points unreservedly to finding ways of sharing development costs and securing the benefits of large-scale production. At the same time we need to keep events under our control in order to preserve a proper balance between national programmes with their associated exports, collaboration and purchase from abroad. At the same time also we need to control the amount and kind of our technology which we allow to pass to potential European competitors and the conditions under which it is passed. The representations made in the National Defence Industries Council and by chairmen of individual firms to individual ministers illustrate the concern which industry feels on these questions.

Collaboration along the lines now envisaged will enable Britain to exert considerable influence over the form of management of projects. The variety of pattern which has been adopted hitherto demonstrates the flexibility which is open to us. In some projects we can take the lead, as with the C.V.R.(T); in others, where the problem of reciprocity is too great to solve by allowing single-nation management, we can share development, as with Jaguar, or set up a joint management organisation, closely controlled as to policy but with delegated powers on day-to-day business, as with the M.R.C.A.; and in others, e.g. helicopters, we can move towards reciprocal procurement.

Quite apart from British participation in the NATO committee structure, we have bilateral committees with most of our potential partners (the exception is Belgium), and in the case of France and Germany a substructure oriented to each of the three Services. This machinery, with which the defence sales organisation is associated, allows us to explore both the operational and technical aspects of collaboration, and the emphasis can be switched from one to the other with suitable representation as occasion demands. The machinery also allows us to keep the collaborative prospects for any project under regular review from the time when the operational requirements are first being discussed to the time when it

passes into production and even beyond. Where lack of resources, financial and physical, is a bar to shared development, a number of countries show no disposition to object –
quite the reverse – to the concept of collaboration through
sales.

The achievements so far have already been listed earlier in
this paper. As to the future, mention has already been made
of the equipment areas on which the Euro-group will concentrate. We intend to supplement this with discussions bilaterally with our main partners on those projects which are of
special concern to them. A number of requirements for major
equipments are likely to arise in the next two or three years,
the cost of which will make the arguments for collaboration
extremely compelling. In one area – battlefield communications – the Euro-group already has some successes to its
credit. Agreement has been reached on the technical parameters to which future systems will conform, thus ensuring
complete interoperability between new systems as they come
into service. In addition to this, encouraging progress has
been made in the preparations for a scheme of reciprocal
procurement in which the various elements of the system can
be shared out between the participating countries for development and production.

The search for collaborative projects and the adaptation of
machinery for exploring possibilities and launching collaborative projects is a continuous process. While it can take
advantage of changes which create easier conditions for collaboration (e.g. United Kingdom entry into the E.E.C.,
developments in the Euro-group), it is not susceptible to
quantum steps in development. Nevertheless, the flexibility
of the system will allow new problems to be considered as
they become relevant to the progress of collaboration and
new methods of consultation to be developed as the political
environment changes.

The emphasis in Britain's collaborative policy so far has
been on bilateral or trilateral effort, and we have used the
international machinery (in effect the NATO machinery) in a
complementary role. We see no reason to make any fundamental change in this balance and it would be wasteful in
effort unnecessarily to duplicate the machinery for informa-

tion exchange which already exists in NATO. Nevertheless, the development of the Euro-group organisation provides a forum in which, without necessarily creating additional committees, appropriate procurement policy questions can be discussed and more generally a climate can be generated in which countries increasingly come to regard collaboration as a sensible way of procuring their equipment.

There are two areas of uncertainty to which continuing attention will have to be paid if equipment collaboration in Europe is to realise its full potential. One is the position of France. So long as France maintains her present attitude towards NATO and the Euro-group, it will be difficult to associate her with the full range of equipment collaboration activities of those bodies. Yet the most comprehensive of our bilateral collaboration programmes is that with France. It is a significant feature of the past few years that, in spite of the changes in the political relations between the two countries, the collaborative programmes have gone ahead undisturbed. All of the 1964/67 generation of collaborative projects have now reached an advanced stage, and the time is now ripe for discussions with France about future cooperation. The signs are that the French are very ready to extend collaboration with us.

The other area of debate is the problem of achieving collaboration at the industrial level. We devote considerable effort towards the harmonisation of military requirements, without which no collaboration can take place, and in spite of the difficulties described earlier, a welcome measure of agreement can often be found. A more intractable problem perhaps is that of ensuring an equitable sharing of the technological and industrial content of collaborative projects. The key to this would seem to lie in the creation of closer transnational associations between firms at present organised on a national basis. The exact pattern will vary from industry to industry. In electronics, where the product range of one firm rarely matches that of any other, association may be relatively loose and *ad hoc*. In aerospace the partnerships may need to be more permanent. The object must be to try to ensure that whatever government launches a project, the technology flowing from it is equitably shared.

Arms procurement is a very complicated process, as is indicated by the problems which so regularly beset us in our national programmes and the wealth of professional advice which has been lavished on the subject in the course of our own reorganisation under the Procurement Executive. It is essential to preserve continuity in this vital field, and in our search for wider co-operation we must be careful not to embark on schemes which are too radical for the system to bear.

The more sensible alternative is to build on what we possess, a process which has no sharply defined starting-point but is all the better for having some firm foundations. In our education of public opinion we can legitimately point to the successes already achieved and the opportunities which are undoubtedly opening out in the Euro-group and elsewhere for further collaboration, but it would be misguided to give the impression that there is some magic formula by which improvements in defence procurement can solve the problems of the alliance.

6

Strategies of European Nations

'CORMORANT'*

The American Obligation

It has been a major objective of the North Atlantic Alliance to involve the Americans in the defence of Europe. It was the United States view from the beginning that, while they must take chief responsibility in the strategic nuclear field and play a large part in naval operations, the 'hard core of ground power in being' would have to come from Europe.[1] To this view they have steadily adhered, and their attitude towards a land force contribution has been coloured accordingly. A presidential message dated 10 March 1955 stated:

> It will be the policy of the United States to continue to maintain in Europe, including Germany, such units of its armed forces as may be necessary and appropriate to constitute its fair share to the forces needed for the joint defence of the North Atlantic Area while a threat to that area exists, and will continue to deploy such forces in accordance with agreed North Atlantic Strategy for the defence of this area.[2]

Everything hinges upon the interpretation of 'fair share'. On their performance up to now it cannot be argued that the Americans have been ungenerous. Their troop strength in

* A senior serving officer in the British Army.
[1] Gen. Omar Bradley, testimony to House of Representatives Committee on Foreign Affairs, Hearings, Mutual Defence Assistance Act of 1949, 81st Congress, 1st Session, p. 71. Quoted in R. N. Rosecranz, *Defence of the Realm* (New York: Columbia Univ. Press, 1968) p. 95.
[2] *Brussels Treaty: Text of the Treaty, the Protocols and Other Documents Concerning the Western European Union* (London: printed for the Western European Union by the Curwen Press, 1961) p. 151.

Germany, which stood at about 275,000 ten years ago, is still about 220,000. Some 35,000 men were returned to the United States in 1967, but a complete set of war equipment for them remains stored in South Germany and their return to Germany is practised under exercise conditions every year. Otherwise the number of formations has not been affected, and in December 1970 President Nixon sent a further message to the North Atlantic Council, then meeting in Brussels, in which he said: 'Given a similar approach by our allies, the United States will maintain and improve its own forces in Europe, and will not reduce them unless there is reciprocal action by our adversaries.'[3]

At first sight nothing could be more specific. The fact is, however, that for upwards of ten years a number of strands in American thinking have been steadily coalescing to produce a climate of opinion in which some reduction of front-line strength in Europe now seems almost inevitable.

In the first place, while there is no compromise in the resolve to oppose any Soviet military threat to Europe, there is a strong tendency to believe that the overwhelming Russian military preponderance of the 1950s no longer holds good. This view assumes that because of the numerous complex problems facing them in Russia, Eastern Europe and China, the Soviets cannot freely capitalise on NATO problems and much of the Soviets' military power must be reserved for other contingencies. Allied to this is the view that the military imbalance of Central Europe has in many cases been misrepresented because of failure to allow for such technical factors as the greater strength and firepower of NATO units, the high ratio of force to space needed for successful attack, the inhibiting effects of tactical nuclear weapons and so forth. On these lines it is possible to argue that NATO has more than enough front-line formations in Germany to do the job.

The second strand of thinking arises from disillusionment with the self-imposed world role of the United States induced by weariness and disappointment in Vietnam. She is now

[3] *NATO Handbook* (Brussels: NATO Information Services, Jan 1971) p. 91.

much less prone to regard herself as a 'nation-state-with-a-mission',[4] and much more willing to take her place as a normal nation-state looking after her own interests in the world.

The third factor is financial. American military expenditure is adding to American foreign exchange problems, even though the Federal Republic undertakes to offset about 80 per cent of foreign exchange costs in Germany by military procurement and various financial measures. The need is becoming urgent to contain the budgetary costs of the European commitment, now estimated at $14 billion a year. Quite apart from pressing domestic needs, there is the problem of converting the American Army onto an all-volunteer basis. The plan involves paying enlistment bonuses and raising the basic pay of recruits by some 50 per cent. The current rate of United States defence spending, at 9 per cent of G.N.P., is more than twice the NATO average. This leaves the Administration very exposed to the charge that America is footing an unfairly high part of the total NATO bill.

It is for this reason that Senator Mansfield has been pressing since 1966 for a big reduction in the size of the United States contribution to NATO. This led in 1971 to his amendment to the normally routine bill which enables conscription to continue, calling for halving of American troop strength in Germany by the end of that year. Although the amendment was defeated, it was generally agreed that the sentiment in Congress has been in Mansfield's favour.

This might suggest that the Americans, on the strength of their contribution in the strategic and tactical nuclear fields, have tended to underrate the importance of conventional forces. In fact the reverse has been the case. It was recognised, even in the Dulles era, that the effectiveness of strategic nuclear weapons was seriously circumscribed and that there was need to be able to meet aggression on equal terms at whatever level it might be offered. With the arrival of Robert McNamara in the Pentagon this view achieved executive momentum. To quote from one of his best-known speeches (September 1967):

[4] John Strachey, *On the Prevention of War* (London: Macmillan, 1962) p. 247.

The fact that the Soviet Union and the United States can mutually destroy one another regardless of who strikes first narrows the range of Soviet aggression which our nuclear forces can effectively deter. Even with our nuclear monopoly in the early post-war period we were unable to deter the Soviet pressure against Berlin, or their support of aggression in Korea. Today our nuclear superiority does not deter all forms of Soviet support of communist insurgency in South East Asia. What all of this has meant is that we, and our allies as well, require substantial non-nuclear forces in order to cope with levels of aggression, that massive strategic forces do not deter. *Thus we and our allies must* maintain substantial conventional forces, fully capable to deal with a wide spectrum of lesser forms of political and military aggression – a level of aggression against which use of strategic nuclear forces would not be to our advantage and thus a level of aggression which these strategic forces by themselves cannot effectively deter.[5]

The strategic implications of this thesis are discussed later. The immediate point to note is that, in parallel with growing pressure within the United States for reduction of their own force contribution, there has been consistent pressure exerted by the United States upon the European allies to fulfil at least their share of the force goals (30 divisions) which they themselves unanimously adopted in the mid-1950s. But these goals have never been met in full and it seems highly unlikely that they ever will be. The following paragraphs explain why this is so.

The German Contribution

Under the Paris Agreements of October 1954 it was agreed that the force levels for the Bundeswehr should not exceed 12 divisions and 1,000 combat aircraft. All should be placed under the Supreme Allied Commander Europe in peace, their

---

[5] Remarks by Secretary of Defence Robert S. McNamara before United Press editors and publishers, San Francisco, Calif, 18 Sep 1967. Quoted in Ralph Lapp, *The Weapons Culture* (New York: Norton, 1968) p. 210. Emphasis added.

location and operational plans to be in accordance with NATO operational concepts and no redeployment or operational use to take place without the consent of SACEUR, subject to political guidance from the North Atlantic Council.[6]

The noteworthy point is that the size of forces stipulated under the Paris Agreements as a maximum has been treated by the Federal German Government as constituting a minimum obligation, and from 1956 the build-up to that total has steadily proceeded. It was decided to enlist men in three categories: regulars; men who would serve from three to fifteen years (*auf Zeit*); and conscripts who would serve for one year only, who were to make up not more than 40 per cent of the total. By 1962 it was found that enlistments *auf Zeit* were lagging and that a one-year period of conscription was unsatisfactory in view of the amount of training needed to cope with modern weapons. Accordingly in 1962 the minimum period of enlistment *auf Zeit* was reduced to two years and the length of the conscription period was increased to eighteen months. Since then the total strength has risen to about 467,000 and the build-up is almost complete.

At its present strength the Bundeswehr is showing clear signs of overstretch. This has shown itself, first and foremost, in the inability of the Army to recruit enough officers and N.C.O.s to serve *auf Zeit*; only about one-half of the officer vacancies are being filled and even so by men serving on very short term. The N.C.O. shortage amounts to some 19,500 against a total N.C.O. strength of 73,000.

The existence of conscription does not in any way relieve this problem; in fact it makes it worse. At present some 93 per cent of all fit young men are called up for service in the Bundeswehr or in one of the authorised alternatives. But about 30 per cent of the whole are declared 'conditionally fit', and are not called up at all. There are clearly many military jobs which they could do, provided care was taken to match the job to the minor disabilities from which they suffer. This was felt to be a grave injustice, and an independent commission under the Vice-President of the Bundestag

---

[6] Protocol on the accession to the North Atlantic Treaty of the Federal Republic of Germany, para. 6.

proposed in 1971[7] to make use of about half the 'conditionally fit' in each age group, without changing the size of the Bundeswehr, by reducing the call-up to fifteen months from 1972. The number of trained soldiers who could be declared to NATO would not be reduced under this proposal, since the length of basic training would be cut from six to four months. This is a rather desperate shift from which two bad consequences follow. First, because technology has advanced to the point where eighteen months' service is the minimum if conscripts are to master the wide field of modern equipment, it follows that the types of jobs which conscripts can satisfactorily carry out will become fewer. Secondly, the training organisation would have to be expanded to cope with the greater throughput of recruits. Both these effects compound the problem of finding enough longer-service soldiers. Nor can it be assumed that, even with the booming economy of Western Germany, there is any enthusiasm for increased expenditure on defence. While the economy is growing at around 5 per cent a year, and the Federal budget is expected to increase by about 6.8 per cent a year, the planned increase of the defence budget is only 2.8 per cent.

Worrying though these problems are, they have been temporarily eclipsed by a crisis in what might be called the social psychology of the Bundeswehr. No nation in history can have tried harder to assimilate the ethos of the armed forces to 'democratic' ideals than have the West Germans since 1950. Great emphasis is placed upon the citizen in uniform whose human dignity and civil rights must be upheld regardless of his duty to obey orders. These attitudes have been institutionalised within the Bundeswehr mainly by the appointment of a Parliamentary Commissioner for the Bundeswehr who deals with some 7,000 cases a year. A further safeguard is provided by the right of soldiers to belong either to a civilian trade union or to the military equivalent, the Bundeswehr Association. Servicemen are also entitled to vote and to stand for election to local and central governments. In taking office the Social Democratic Government introduced regular discussion meetings with all ranks from generals to

[7] 'Wehrgerechtigkeit in der Bundesrepublik Deutschland', Wehrstruktur Kommission der Bundesregierung, 3 Feb 1971.

N.C.O.s. In short, the anti-authoritarianism which the Bundesrepublik itself has endorsed is being implanted deliberately within the Bundeswehr. The 1970 White Paper sums up the position as follows: 'A democratic society, through the media of legislation, government and parliamentary control, sets up the armed forces consonant with its principles and assigns them their missions. In short the nation is the school of the army and not vice versa.'[8]

These admirable sentiments sort ill with German military traditions and not surprisingly a form of mental chaos has resulted. The most recent report of the Parliamentary Commissioner concluded that discipline and morale are weak. He complained of conscientious objectors approaching 20,000 a year, portraits of Che, Mao and Lenin adorning barrack-room lockers, and the growing consumption of soft drugs.[9] While it would be quite wrong to conclude that the Bundeswehr is on the verge of disintegrating, what has been said shows sufficient reasons why any expansion of the numbers of German divisions assigned to SACEUR is impossible.

The French Contribution

For nearly twenty years the French played a leading part in providing for the collective defence of north-west Europe. But from the time of his access to power in 1958, de Gaulle's dislike of NATO became evident. In 1050 he withdrew the French fleet from NATO. In 1960 he refused to allow nuclear weapons to be stocked in France for American fighter bombers. Thereafter he continued to seek means to emphasise his independence of the Atlantic connection and to consolidate (as he hoped) the dominant position of France.

Theoretical underpinning was provided by his Chief of Defence Staff, General Ailleret, in a very interesting article published in the *Revue de Défense Nationale* in September 1964.[10] He examined two possible ways of defending Europe against a large-scale conventional attack. One way, he said, would be by a purely conventional defence – accepting a

[8] German White Paper on Defence, 1970 (English-language version) p. 120.   [9] *Economist*, 27 Mar 1971, p. 30.
[10] *Survival* (Nov–Dec 1964) pp. 258–65.

numerical inferiority of at least 3:2, and greater if both sides
had time to reinforce beforehand. He agreed that this might
work, but only if a great deal of ground was surrendered,
thus taking advantage of attrition upon the enemy and the
ever-increasing distance from his base. Logistic and communications infrastructure in the area abandoned to the
enemy would have to be utterly destroyed. He argued that
this was quite incompatible with a forward strategy: 'If the
Russians can be stopped we should congratulate ourselves if
it were done on the Rhine. The Somme, the Aisne, the
Vosges, the Jura and the Alps would be more likely.' Bearing
in mind the uncertainty of reconquest, for a very long time
if at all, he dismissed this solution. As an alternative he discussed the possibility of a defensive battle using tactical
nuclear weapons – if the enemy used them first or could not
otherwise be prevented from deep penetration. This he also
accepted as a feasible method, but he argued on the analogy
of the octopus that one would have not only to strike and
halt the tentacles but also to puncture the body. This would
entail, in his view, nuclear interdiction up to a depth of 900
miles on either side of the battle line. A great number of
kilotons would have to be fired, at troops, nuclear delivery
means and logistic facilities, into an area containing many
more civilians than soldiers. The result would be to wipe out
Europe, over a depth of 1,800 miles, from the Atlantic to the
Soviet frontier. Western forces must, he said, 'be prepared for
this hypothesis both intellectually and materially; but it is one'
which they could not recommend, only resign themselves to'.

This left, in his view, only one acceptable solution. In the
event of any real aggression, nuclear bombs must be dropped
on the strategic war potential of the aggressor. The action of
the land/air forces would then be as follows. They would
set up along the regions to be protected a defensive line
designed *not* to halt powerful attack but simply 'to measure
the minimum level of enemy attack having the characteristics
of such aggression as would bring the nuclear defensive
strategy into play'. Only a limited number of divisions would
then be needed in the front line. 'Others could be placed in
reserve in the depth of the theatre of operations ready to
carry out decidedly offensive counter-attacks aimed at wiping

out any deep penetration the enemy may make.' General Ailleret recognised that the automatic tripwire effect of breaking the forward line would operate in practice and in anticipation only if it were believed in and accepted by everyone, including the Soviets, regardless of the consequences. This was a crucial difficulty because, while Ailleret's thinking no doubt chimed well with de Gaulle's, it ran clear counter to the tide of opinion in NATO which was moving irresistibly towards a much less cut-and-dried conception.

This provided de Gaulle with the excuse he required. Since there was no chance of influencing NATO in general, and the Americans in particular, towards a reversion to the tripwire type of strategy, and since France had by this time a national strategic capability of her own, it could be represented as a logical consequence that France should withdraw from the integrated structure of NATO and thus become free to operate her own strategy. In 1966 he gave formal notice that France would dissociate from the headquarters structure of NATO and cease to assign forces from July of the same year. He made it clear that the North Atlantic Treaty itself was not in question, nor the stationing of two divisions of the *Forces de Manœuvre* in Germany (the whole force consisted of five mechanised divisions, three in north-east France and two in Germany), and that liaison with the NATO headquarters was to continue. The effects upon the French forces themselves have been comparatively slight. The Honest John rockets and aircraft bombs lost their American nuclear warheads, and their French equivalents in the shape of bombs for the Mirage IIIE and Pluton have recently entered service and are expected in service in 1973–4, respectively. But French forces have continued to take part in exercises in Germany and the role of the two French divisions remained always what it has been and what was excellently described by General Ailleret, 'to carry out decidedly offensive counter-attacks aimed at wiping out any deep penetration'.

The role of the remainder of the *Forces de Manœuvre* in north-east France was described by General Fourquet, General Ailleret's successor, in a speech to the Institut des Hautes Études de Défense Nationale in March 1969.[11] He

11 *Survival* (July 1969) pp. 206–11.

accorded first priority to the protection of the strategic nuclear forces (silos and air bases), their associated head-quarters and the seat of government. He expounded a theory of the land–air battle differing in detail only from his pre-decessor's but with a novel emphasis. The *Forces de Manœuvre* could, he thought, by mobility and flexibility and with good air cover, 'deal with minor action for as long as required while retaining its ability to fulfil a nuclear role before the level of a strategic exchange is reached'. He stressed the impossibility of holding a continuous front and the offensive nature of the action, although it might take place 'only a short distance from our frontier while profiting as much as possible from the earlier efforts of our allies'. But the essential point, he thought, 'was to test the enemy's inten-tion, so as not to unleash the strategic strike prematurely, and thus make clear our will to resist without indulging in the game of escalation'. If this sounds like a rather cynical ex-ploitation of France's geographical position and somewhat short on logic, a recent comment by General Beaufre may be apropos: 'We think that by stepping out of the game and by having our own position we increase the deterrent position because we *raise a doubt about our rationality*.'[12]

In producing the forces to implement this policy the French, like the Germans, have come up against ineluctable problems both of manpower and finance. The proportion of French defence expenditure has declined from 5.6 per cent of the G.N.P. in 1961 to 3.39 per cent in 1970. By 1975 it will have declined still further to around 3 per cent, according to the latest *Loi de Programme*. Under the manning principle according to which the French armed forces are raised, all able-bodied men are required to serve. Changes in the man-ning requirement have therefore to be accommodated by changing the duration of conscriptive service. Since the end of the Algerian war the French armed forces ran down in strength from just over a million to just under half a million, the period of conscription being dropped by stages from twenty-eight to sixteen months. The percentage of conscripts

---

[12] Gen. Beaufre, 'French Defence Policy', lecture to the Royal United Services Institute, 29 Oct 1961, reprinted in *R.U.S.I. Journal* (Mar 1970) p. 9. Emphasis added.

dropped from 60 per cent in 1960 to about 52 per cent in 1970. Thus the number of conscripts was reduced by rather more than half while the period of conscription dropped by rather less than half. The difference was taken up partly by stiffening medical standards, allowing exemption for social hardship and admitting conscientious objectors, and partly by calling up only about two-thirds of the young men available in any one year and carrying forward the remainder. The age of call-up has thus risen by about four months in each year and by April 1970 had reached about twenty years and five months on average. Clearly this process could not continue indefinitely.

A further difficulty arose over the deferment system which applied to any young man undergoing further education provided he continued to pass his examinations. This affected no less than 110,000 out of an age group of 440,000 in 1969 and in another five years might well have risen to twice that number. The inconvenience of a deferment policy on this scale is substantial. First, it can be represented as a form of unfair discrimination – 'une invention de la classe bourgeoise et un moyen de pression efficace'.[13] The genuine grievance upon which this slogan is based arises from the very low pay of the conscript,[14] which arguably bears most heavily upon the less able young men called up early rather than upon their cleverer and older comrades in arms. Secondly, the mixing of young men of widely different ages in the same barrack room, and the feeling on the part of graduates that their talents are underemployed, makes for further disharmony. And the fact that, of any given age group, only some 45 per cent were being called up at the normal time did not give the impression of being a fair system.

Thus in France, as in Germany, the need to secure equity in conscription has become overriding. In June 1970 the French National Assembly gave overwhelming approval to a bill providing for the principle of universal military training to be maintained by cutting the length of conscript service to twelve months, from November of that year. The

[13] Jacques Isnard, 'La réforme du service nationale', *Le Monde*, 6 June 1970, quoting the National Union of French Students (UNEF).
[14] 75 centimes a day plus some wine and cigarettes.

deferment system has also been radically curtailed. The normal age of call-up will in future be nineteen years, but all may choose to be called up either as early as eighteen or as late as twenty-one so that their year with the colours can be dove-tailed with their further education.

As in Germany, a high price will be paid for this measure both in terms of training problems and in higher running expenses. The greater throughput of conscripts has been estimated to cost a further 150 million francs a year, and the cost of attracting sufficiently high-grade long-term service men to train them and to man the more complex equipment has been quoted as 1,000 million francs. This additional manpower cost is a grave embarrassment and has been tackled by the arbitrary decision to run down the overall strength of manpower (military and civilian) at the rate of from 1–2 per cent a year. This will mean a loss over a five-year period of some 12,000–13,000 long-term servicemen. The effects of this, coming on top of the reduction in length of conscript service, cast a large question mark over the combat effectiveness of the forces.

In 1966 General Steinhoff, then recently Chief of Staff to the Allied Air Forces Central Europe, described the manpower and equipment of the French Army units as leaving 'much to be desired by comparison with NATO standards'.[15] Since then they have not been subject to NATO formal inspection. Re-equipment has gone steadily ahead, but the problems of manning and training these formations – particularly those in France which do not exercise in Germany – have steadily become more difficult. For all practical purposes, therefore, while the two divisions in Germany can be counted as a useful bonus on the NATO side, any discussion of the remaining three divisions of the *Forces de Manœuvre* in terms of additional force contributions is entirely academic – whether the French are persuaded to return to the military structures of NATO or not. The real significance of these divisions is, and always has been, in the field of home defence and internal security. Though they may be equipped for mobile operations in north-west Europe, there is no prospect of their being manned or trained to any pur-

15 *Europa Archiv*, 10 Aug 1966; *Survival* (Nov 1966) p. 367.

pose other than operations within the boundaries of France. As things stand at present there is good reason to expect a reduction in the total strength of the field Army,[16] and no increase is even remotely probable.

The British Contribution

In the early 1950s British support of NATO was generous almost to the point of imprudence. As part of the arrangements to incorporate the German forces into NATO through membership of an expanded Western European Union, Britain undertook to maintain on the continent of Europe 'four divisions and the Second Tactical Air Force, or such other forces as the Supreme Allied Commander Europe considers as having equivalent fighting capacity'. She further promised 'not to withdraw these forces against the wishes of the majority of the High Contracting Parties who should take their decision in the knowledge of the views of the Supreme Allied Commander Europe'. The undertaking would not be binding in the event of 'an acute overseas emergency'; and if the maintenance of the forces were to throw too great a strain on external finances, the North Atlantic Council would be asked to review the financial conditions on which these forces were maintained.[17]

Within two years the waiver had been invoked. In 1956 application was made to the Council of the Western European Union who acquiesced in a reduction in strength of the British Army of the Rhine from 77,000 to 64,000 in 1957–8 and to 55,000 in the following year. Over the same period the aircraft of the Second Tactical Air Force were reduced by about one-half. Although suggestions of further drastic reductions were made at the time, these were not proceeded with and the commitment has remained ever since at the figure of 55,000 men.

During the 1960s the British attitude to the problem of NATO force goals was coloured by the belief that sufficient

[16] A first step has already been seen in the reduction of the 11th Intervention Division by 1,800 men and the relegation of one brigade (the 9th) to a home defence role. *Le Monde*, 8 July 1971.

[17] Protocol No. II on the Forces of the Western European Union, Article VI, 23 Oct 1954.

ground formations were already available and that, rather than adhere to obsolete targets, strategy should be designed to fit the forces which national governments were prepared to provide. It was only in the aftermath of devaluation, early in 1968, that any substantial alternatives came under discussion, and even so they were two-edged. On the one hand, the obvious need to economise on foreign exchange led to the decision to redeploy one brigade to the United Kingdom. On the other hand, accelerated withdrawals from various overseas commitments made it possible to contemplate a more specific commitment of the strategic reserve in the United Kingdom. A division of three infantry brigades, a parachute force and one Special Air Service regiment were earmarked for assignment to NATO.

In 1970 the Labour Government stationed additional air-defence squadrons on the Continent and arranged for the permanent return to Germany of the brigade 'redeployed' to the United Kingdom two years earlier. The Conservative Government, later in the same year, announced plans for further increases which included an additional armoured-car regiment from the Reserve Army, and four squadrons of R.A.F. offensive support aircraft (Jaguar) to be made available to SACEUR. But these welcome additions have to some extent been offset by temporary withdrawals to meet the emergency which broke out in Ulster in August 1969.

The Military Balance

The situation to be faced, therefore, is this. At a time when there is much talk of détente and heavy pressure from domestic social programmes, governments in the United States, Germany, France and Britain all alike will find it difficult, however good their intentions, to increase their military contribution to Western defence. It is of course possible that events either in Eastern or Western Europe or elsewhere might cause a scare so great as to set off a major reversal of policy and general force increases. The Korean war had this effect. Crises in Berlin, Cuba and Czechoslovakia did not. Such an event is by definition unpredictable and no argument can be hung upon it. But barring discontinuities of this nature, the expectation is that NATO will have to live within its existing means and indeed accommodate to some decline in front-line strength within the foreseeable future. Before discussing how this might be done, it is necesary to review briefly the existing military balance, and the strategy which has been devised in the light of it.

At first sight there is a comforting symmetry between the 25 Allied divisions and 2,000 or so tactical aircraft in West Germany and Holland on the one hand, and the 25 Soviet divisions and 2,400 tactical aircraft in East Germany and Czechoslovakia on the other. The comparison becomes even more reassuring when note is taken of the greater strength of NATO divisions, the greater capability of NATO aircraft and the 2:1 superiority of tactical nuclear warheads. There are, however, important factors tipping the balance the other way. First, if the loyalty of non-Soviet forces of the Warsaw Pact could be assured and their presence not required for internal security, then there would be twice the number of divisions available to the Pact and the number of tactical aircraft substantially increased. The Warsaw Pact's preponderance in tanks (2:1) and air-defence aircraft (8:1) becomes particularly marked. Second, the Warsaw Pact has far greater reinforcement capability. There are some 28 Russian divisions west of the Urals, and their movement capacity has been quoted as between 5 and 10 divisions per day. The Americans, by contrast, would take up to thirty days to return the two 'redeployed' brigades, and the arrival of two further earmarked divisions (whatever allowance be made for the C.5 aircraft) would clearly take longer. To this could be added at most two reserve divisions from the Low Countries, the British Strategic Reserve (1⅓ divisions), one Canadian brigade, and from the United States in due course a further three regular and eight National Guard divisions. The latter are all either of doubtful quality or primarily equipped for other theatres or only partly trained. On the most favourable assumption, NATO could add only another 15 divisions to its order of battle, and that only in a matter of months. For these reasons it is assumed that, after reinforcement, NATO would have to fight outnumbered by land and air in the ratio of between 1:2 and 1:3. Finally, the Warsaw Pact forces enjoy the advantages of much greater homogeneity and standard-isation, and to the extent that they would hold the strategic initiative and could concentrate upon the lines of the *glavnyi udar* – the 'main blow' – they could obtain local superiority of 5:1 or even more.

The Strategy of Flexible Response

The best form of deterrence consists in having the ability to fight *and win* whatever type of engagement might ensue if deterrence failed. It is clear that NATO has such a capability over a wide band of the defence spectrum, which would include border incidents, *coup de main* operations against limited objectives within West Germany, and even an invasion on the scale of that mounted against Czechoslovakia in 1968 with or without the use of the tactical nuclear weapons. There is also balance of a kind, at the level of a strategic nuclear interchange. The level at which an equal and opposite response can *not* be offered is precisely that which NATO has always adopted as the 'worst case' on which to base its main contingency plans – that is, a massive attack by the Warsaw Pact after reinforcement. The doctrine evolved in the mid-1950s to meet this contingency involved NATO taking the initiative in the use of nuclear weapons 'at the outset'. The centrepiece of this initiative lay in SACEUR's nuclear strike plan, which involved all available aircraft and medium-range missiles, supplemented from 1963 onwards by the British V-bomber force and three American Polaris submarines. Their task was to eliminate the attacking power's military potential, lines of communication and supply dumps at one blow. Aircraft and missiles would go into action under an automatic contingency plan worked out in advance, assuming of course that political consent had been granted. It was assumed that this would be forthcoming very early and that all aircraft could set off on their one and only mission within the first few hours of a major invasion, otherwise they would all have been destroyed on the ground. This strategy lasted from 1957 to 1967, but the dangers and problems resulting from it had been known for a considerable period. In 1958 Admiral Brown, Commander-in-Chief Allied Forces

Southern Europe, pointed out that there was no dependable distinction between tactical and strategic situations.[18] Helmut Schmidt pointed out[19] that the Soviet Missile Command might well respond to attacks on the Vistula bridges involving widespread devastation of Warsaw by destroying the Elbe and Rhine crossings and in so doing produce similar devastation in Hamburg, Cologne and Düsseldorf. More recently a team of scientists, headed by Profesor Carl Fredrich von Weiszäcker, concluded that twenty 2-megaton bombs exploded over Western Germany would claim 10 million dead, and 200 bombs would be enough to destroy 50 million West Germans.[20]

The strategy known as 'flexible response' was evolved in an attempt to mitigate the rigour and escape the consequences of this doctrine. This concept allows the allies to respond in a controlled and adequate manner in the event of a crisis or an attack:

> The first principle is to meet any aggression with direct defence at approximately the same level and the second is to deter through the possibility of escalation. . . . The keystone of the new strategy is that an aggressor must be convinced of NATO's readiness to use nuclear weapons if necessary, but at the same time he must be uncertain regarding the timings or the circumstances on which they would be used.[21]

This strategy depends critically, according to the British White Paper of 1970, on maintaining conventional forces in Western Europe at a level 'which will give NATO an alternative to a nuclear response against anything but a major deliberate attack; and which, if an attack on this scale should occur, would allow time for negotiation to end the conflict and for consultation among the allies about the initial use of

---

[18] Quoted by Fred Mulley, *The Politics of Western Defence* (London, 1962) p. 99.
[19] Helmut Schmidt, *Defence or Retaliation* (Edinburgh: Oliver & Boyd, 1962) p. 99.
[20] 'Consequences of War and Prevention of War', quoted in *Süddeutsche Zeitung*, 16 Dec 1970.
[21] German White Paper on Defence, 1970, pp. 28–9.

nuclear weapons if negotiations should fail'.[22] This formu-
lation invites two further questions: how much time is to be
allowed, and how large a force is needed to secure it? West
Germany is a shallow country along an east–west axis and
could be overrun at the Soviets' normative rate of advance in
two to four days. On the other hand, no one can suppose that
negotiations involving fifteen sovereign governments covering the initial use of nuclear weapons could be conducted
quickly. In Denis Healey's view, the period of time available
for consultation is unlikely to be more than a 'very few days;
it is more likely to be under five than under ten'.[23] But for
that length of time he believes that NATO is capable of
stemming an enemy aggression close to the eastern border of
the Federal Republic without using any nuclear weapons at
all.[24] This clearly implies the existence of forces on the ground
and in the air large enough to hold some form of continuous
line on the Central Front and with sufficient reserves to provide some depth. 'At present the level of these conventional
forces is *just sufficient* for this purpose.'[25]

Undoubtedly this doctrine makes the prospect of attacking
Europe a very uninviting one to the Soviets, if only because,
to quote Denis Healey once more, 'no rational Soviet government would stake the survival of the Russian people on the
guess that, in the event, the United States government would
prefer to see its allies occupied and the American Army in
Europe destroyed rather than raise the level of the conflict'.[26]
The decision to initiate nuclear war would be a heavy one to
take for the NATO governments, and the recognition of its
far-reaching consequences lay behind NATO's switch to a
strategy of flexible response. But the Russians are unlikely to
be much swayed by any such assessment of NATO's intentions. They look rather at the forces available on the ground
and almost certainly make the assumption that nuclear
weapons would be used in the event of any major aggression.
On this basis it is possible to argue that the mere existence of

---

[22] British Defence White Paper, Cmnd 4290 (1970) pp. 5, 6.
[23] 'Does the Strategy of Flexible Response Need Modifying?', R.U.S.I.
discussion, 4 Nov 1970, p. 1.   [24] Interview with *Die Welt*, 27 May 1970.
[25] British Defence White Paper, 1970, p. 6. Emphasis added.
[26] 'On European Defence', 6th International Wehrkunde Meeting,
1–2 July 1969, in *Survival* (Apr 1969) p. 110.

these weapons is a sufficient deterrent and the role of conventional forces is largely symbolic. This leads to a line of thinking which attaches little importance to disparities in the military balance between East and West. Thus Denis Healey has argued: 'Fortunately, like the strategic nuclear balance, the stability of military balance in Europe can tolerate larger fluctuations in relative force capability than General Staffs will readily admit.'[27] General Beaufre considers that the ability to implement one's declared strategy is unimportant since the latter 'is just like bluffing at cards'.[28] But the analogy with poker is incomplete if it is confined to the psychological impact upon the opponent. Given that a major deliberate attack by the Soviets on the Central Front is a most improbable contingency; given therefore that the political self-confidence of the nations of Western Europe is the chief object to be defended, how much actual defensive capability do these nations need? The answer is that they need sufficient to ensure that there is no military option open to the potential enemy which would offer him the chance of quick and unassailable gains and leave the West with literally no effective response. If such an option lay open, quite regardless of how attractive it might or might not appear to the adversary, this would be likely to erode the psychological defences of the West to the point where the will to defend by any means would come in doubt, cohesion would waste away and the countries would travel their separate ways towards the status presently enjoyed by Finland.

This brings us back, therefore, to the problem of defence on the Central Front, the contention that this depends critically on maintaining a certain level of land and air forces, and that the present level of forces is 'just sufficient'.[29] Admittedly, any assessment of the military balance is imprecise,

[27] 'Deluded Strategies in the Twilight of the Cold War', *The Times*, 2 Mar 1971.   [28] 'French Defence Policy', pp. 5, 9.

[29] British Defence White Paper, 1970, para. 55. See also Gen. Sir John Hackett, 'When Defence Falls Short', *Sunday Times*, 1 Mar 1970: 'In my opinion CINCENT may have just enough to be free from an absolute requirement for a very early release'; and Gen. A. J. Goodpaster, 'The Defence of Europe', *R.U.S.I. Journal* (Mar 1971) pp. 34, 35, 39: 'Our sharpest concern is any tendency towards reduction or redeployment of forces withdrawing them from forward areas when they can best contribute to forward defence. We have exhausted our margin for such cuts.'

with many unknowns and some unknowables. But as Denis Healey himself says: 'Any important reduction in the total number of forces would make the strategy doubtful at every level from the top down to the chaps in the front line.'[30] Here is the rub. When it comes to laying out troops in defensive positions on the ground, the range of weapons, the nature of the terrain and above all the fact that more than half the year is spent in darkness or in fog sets a limit to the frontage that any formation can credibly defend – beyond which the concept of a continuous defence with reserves in depth becomes a manifest absurdity. On the North German plain, if due allowance is made for reserves, a forward division is responsible for a frontage of 20 miles. This is coming close to the practical limit regardless of the relativities of force levels on either side. If force levels are already close to the lower limit below which the strategy of flexible response in its present form becomes unworkable, and if reductions in these force levels are highly probable within the foreseeable future, how is the situation to be contained? It is fashionable to suggest that European defence co-operation and mutual and balanced force reductions (M.B.F.R.) might help to solve this problem.

Space does not admit a discussion of these topics. On the first it must suffice to say that no development in European defence co-operation in itself makes the allocation of greater resources by government for defence either more or less probable. On the M.B.F.R. negotiations two things can be said with some confidence. First, there is no pressure in prospect which could force the Russians into accepting any scale of troop reductions which would threaten either their political control in Eastern Europe or their ability to reinforce heavily with Soviet forces if the need arose. Second, the pressures for troop reductions, particularly in America and Germany, are such that an M.B.F.R. agreement might well have to provide a public relations cloak for reductions that had become inevitable in any case. Such reductions, if not at the 'symbolic' then certainly at the 'substantial' stage, must prove the last straw and serve to make the present strategy unworkable.

[30] 'Does the Strategy of Flexible Response Need Modifying', p. 2.

It has been suggested that it would be possible to increase the efficiency of the military instrument by redeploying forces so as to increase the delaying power or deterrent effect of NATO. This could be done either by changing the distribution of national forces along the front or by redistributing them as between front-line forces and reserves in depth, or simply by reforming them into more and smaller formations. The most persuasive suggestion would be to withdraw the American divisions into a central reserve. The southern sector of the front, where they are now concentrated, is the most easily defensible and could stand some weakening. A reserve role could enable them to capitalise upon mobility, particularly in the air cavalry mode developed in Vietnam, and have the great political advantage of involving the Americans in the repulse of any incursion regardless of where on the front it took place. In itself, however, such redeployment could have only a marginal influence upon the delaying power of NATO forces and thus upon future shortfalls in force levels.

It has also been suggested that military effectiveness will be improved since the balance of advantage in conventional weapons is still swinging in favour of the defence – both against tanks and aircraft. In the case of anti-aircraft defence it is certainly true that the development of surface-to-air missiles for use against low-flying attackers shows great promise – but not to the extent of redressing the West's inferiority in interceptor aircraft, let alone to deny local air superiority to the enemy when he chooses to exercise it. Allied mechanised movement on any scale will still be restricted, therefore, to the hours of darkness and poor visibility. In the case of anti-tank weaponry the argument rests upon a number of technical developments – mainly of tank destroyers, wire-guided missiles, including those carried on helicopters, and indirect-fire weapons. The tank destroyer is a proven German concept and its effects are less revolutionary than some of its proponents would suggest. Wire-guided missiles, now present in growing quantities, have reputedly been successful in Vietnam, but the survivability of helicopters has not yet been fully demonstrated in European conditions. The indirect-fire weapons – anti-tank mines and hollow-charge bombs scattered by guns, rockets and aircraft – are still in the stage of research and development. These systems offer the advantage of relative cheapness with flexibility and the prospect of high attrition rates. But their more extreme enthusiasts tend to overlook probable developments in tank design, in such fields as armour protection, low silhouette and target acquisition devices. It is certainly too early to say that the strategic balance will be significantly redressed by technical developments in anti-tank warfare within this decade.[31]

A New Defence Policy for NATO

It remains to examine one further alternative development, the main outlines of which are now beginning to emerge and which could offer, during the later years of this decade, a far more consistent and satisfactory strategy than any that has gone before. It has been the burden of this paper that future plans must take into account three apparent irreconcilables: forward defence because a conventional withdrawal action fought in great depth is incompatible with the political aim; a diminished scale of front-line regular formations such that linear defence of the whole front will no longer be possible, given the obvious need for adequate reserves, and recognition of the grave implications of the first use of tactical nuclear weapons. How can these be harmonised?

In the early days of planning for West German rearmament, in 1954, a plan was floated by Colonel Bogislav von Bonin whereby the German Army would have consisted of an all-volunteer force, about 150,000 strong, equipped with 8,000 anti-tank guns and formed into defensive units for deployment as a continuous screen within 50 km of the zonal border. They would form a covering force behind which mobile allied forces could mount their counter-attacks. The linear character of the proposed screen was an obvious weakness of this concept, but this idea of a semi-static matrix of local defences was picked up and given more precision by Liddell Hart in the early 1960s:

[31] Trevor Cliffe, *Military Technology and the European Defence*, Adelphi Paper No. 89 (London: International Institute for Strategic Studies, 1972).

The required number of divisions would be somewhat less if there was a citizen militia, of the Swiss type, available to man a deep network of defence posts in the forward zone – as a means of helping to delay the enemy's advance while the divisions of the mobile reserve converged upon the threatened sectors. This militia would need to be so organised that the posts could be manned at short notice by militia men living or working nearby. It would also be desirable to have such a militia available in the rear area as a check on the enemy airborne descent to secure key-points there and to block the countermoves of the NATO mobile division.

If a militia force of this kind was available for local defence the requirement for the main shield force might be reduced from twenty-six to twenty divisions – that is a 1 to 2 basis versus the enemy's possible maximum in a surprise offensive on the Central Europe front.[32]

He considered that a force of this level would be a much better shield, particularly if the mobile divisions were all-regular, and that they could keep in check a Soviet attack without the use of atomic weapons.

This idea, after a ten-year time-lag, is now beginning to bite. A recent very thoughtful article by two acknowledged tactical experts has amplified Liddell Hart's idea in terms of the following concept adapted to the Central Front:[33]

(a) To conduct vigorous guerrilla operations in selected areas of close terrain (they mention twenty-three such areas east of the Rhine but excluding the Ruhr).

(b) To conduct a mobile defence with mechanised forces deployed in depth along open approaches and using the guerrilla area as pivots.

(c) To strike through the guerrilla areas at the enemy flanks and rear with small armoured groups.

Both guerrilla and mechanised forces would act to a single co-ordinated and mutually supporting plan, the aim of the

[32] Sir Basil Liddell Hart, *Deterrent or Defence* (London: Stevens, 1960) pp. 165–73.

[33] Brig. D. M. Pomtifex and Lieut.-Col. E. A. Burgess, in *British Army Review*, no. 35 (Aug 1970).

guerrillas in essence being to impose delay and attrition on the enemy if he tried to go through their area, or to canalise him into the main approaches where the mechanised forces will be deployed to meet him. Moreover, by establishing strongholds in depth the enemy is denied undisputed control of any occupied territory and thus gains no quick result – no *fait accompli*. The guerrillas themselves could be formed up from specially trained reservists – 'a force with local knowledge but without deep local responsibilities' – armed with an efficient light anti-tank weapon (of the disposable rocket-launcher variety) and a hand-held anti-aircraft weapon such as Blowpipe. The majority would clearly be German, but the advantage of providing a proportion from other NATO countries is obvious: they would presumably have to be regular commando or parachute units. In the forward area the authors have calculated the numerical requirement as 15,000 West German and ten NATO regular units.

At first sight this seems too good to be true. Can it be feasible to retain tactical control with fewer front-line regular troops; to obtain depth of manoeuvre without surrendering territory; to make the occupation of NATO territory thoroughly unattractive without resorting to threats of nuclear warfare? Second thoughts suggest that this might be the case, and the concept has gathered both momentum and support from such weighty authorities as Sir Walter Walker and Sir John Slessor.[34] Denis Healey has spoken in its support.[35] Perhaps more important is the fact that the Germans are moving in this direction. A tentative first step is being taken in the current conversion of six brigades to the 'Jäger' role. These contain no tanks or armoured personnel carriers, but are motorised, with strong tank-destroyer elements and high dismounted strength. They are to be grouped into three divisions: at Marburg in Hesse, Regensburg in the Bavarian forest and the Mountain Division at Garmisch. Their role is mobile defence in the wooded uplands, and one of their most revolutionary features is the fact that each company contains a reservist platoon and each brigade a reservist battalion.

[34] Gen. Sir Walter Walker, lectures to Oslo Military Society, 7 Dec 1970 (unpublished); Sir John Slessor, letter to the *Economist*, 12 Dec 1970.
[35] 'Does the Strategy of Flexible Response Need Modifying?', p. 2.

More to the point is the fact that the Manpower Structure Commission has now formally recommended that the West German Army of the 1980s should be a two-tier one: part fully professional volunteer regulars and part militia similar to the Swiss and Swedish models.[36] A similar notion floated by General Georges Picot in France is said to have found favour with M. Debré.[37] The British Army is all-regular now, and by 1980 the American Army almost certainly will be. The fulfilment of Liddell Hart's concept might not then be so far off.

[36] *Frankfurter Allgemeine*, 13 Aug 1971. [37] *Die Welt*, 8 Oct 1970.

Index